DuPont Forest

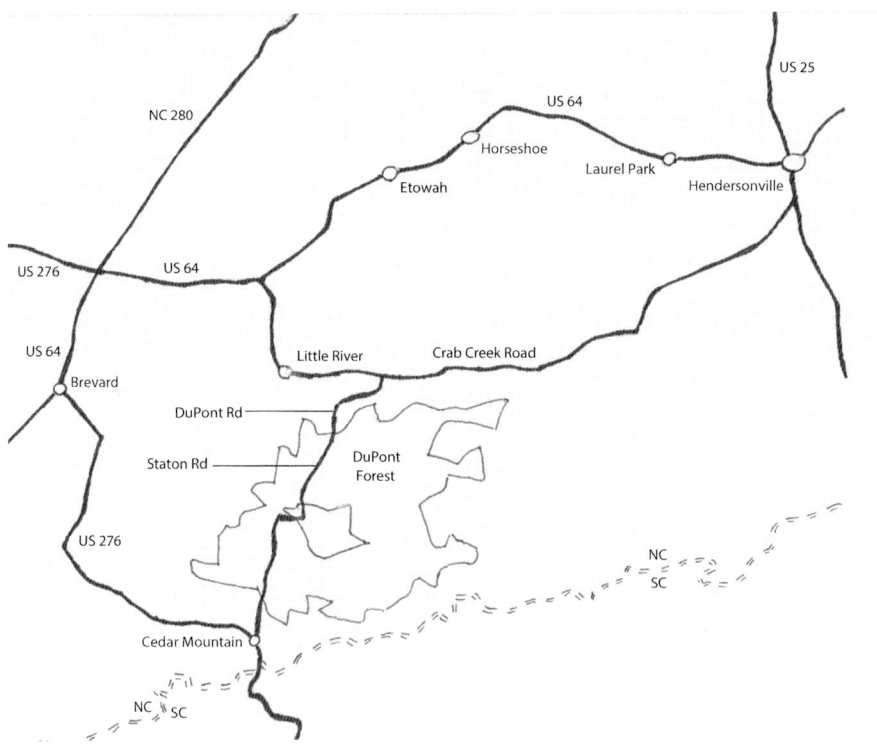

Map of the DuPont Forest area. *Courtesy of Diane Jacqmin.*

DuPont Forest
A History

DANNY BERNSTEIN

Published by The History Press
Charleston, SC
www.historypress.com

Copyright © 2020 by Danny Bernstein
All rights reserved

First published 2020

Manufactured in the United States

ISBN 9781467146883

Library of Congress Control Number: 2020938472

Notice: The information in this book is true and complete to the best of our knowledge. It is offered without guarantee on the part of the author or The History Press. The author and The History Press disclaim all liability in connection with the use of this book.

All rights reserved. No part of this book may be reproduced or transmitted in any form whatsoever without prior written permission from the publisher except in the case of brief quotations embodied in critical articles and reviews.

*To the memory of Lenny Bernstein,
who first said that DuPont Forest is a story waiting to be told.*

Contents

Acknowledgements   11
Cast of Major Characters   13

PART I: EXPLORING THE FOREST
Why DuPont Forest?   15
Recalling a Buck Forest Childhood   18
What Is in DuPont Forest Today   22

PART II: SETTLERS AND LAND BARONS
Meeting the First Settlers   25
Visiting the Land of the Sky   29
Kingdom of the Happy Land   32
Finding Cherokee Petroglyphs   33
Growing Up in Cedar Mountain   35
Creating Buck Forest Lodge   37
Hike: Three Waterfalls in Three Miles   42
Who Was Alex Guion?   47
Appalachians Make Good Workers   49

PART III: DUPONT CORPORATION GOES TO WORK
Immigrant Irénée Starts an Empire   53
DuPont Corporation Comes to Western North Carolina   56
Channing Hubbard, the First Site Employee   61

CONTENTS

Making Hyperpure Silicon   64
What to Do with All This Land?   66
Moving on to X-Ray Film   72
Earle Johnson Remembers   75
Exploring the Twists and Turns of Cascade Lake Road   79
Lewis Staton Gets a Road   82
Hike: Spring in DuPont Forest   84
Brevard, Past and Present, with Stuart English   88
The DuPont Plant Was a Good Place to Work   91

PART IV: SUMMIT CAMPS
Summer Camp, the Best Part of Childhood   93
Airstrip Trail   100
Buck Forest Development   102

PART V: END OF AN ERA
Growing Up DuPont   105
DuPont Corporation Sells the Plant   109
Hike: Midsummer Walk from Guion Farm   112
Fight for the Falls   116
Alan Hirsch Remembers the Fight for the Waterfalls   119
Aleen Steinberg, Environmental Activist   121
Fauna and Flora in the Forest   124
Jeff Jennings Saves a Forest   127
The X-Ray Plant Closes   129

PART VI: THE FOREST GROWS UP
Dave Brown, First Forest Supervisor   133
Hike: Bewildered on Sheep Mountain Trail   135
Studying the Forest Management Plan   138
Creating a Recreational Forest   142
We Can All Get Along   143
Speaking with Forest Supervisor Jason Guidry   148
Hike: Walking Joanna Road from Both Directions   150
Blockbusters in the Forest   153
Visiting the Donut Hole   156
Holmes Educational State Forest: DuPont Forest's Smaller Friend   160

Contents

Part VII: The Future of DuPont Forest
Pay to Play in the Forest?   165
Kiwi Gelato in Brevard   167
Marielle DeJong Comes Home   170
Contemplations and Speculations   172
DuPont Forest Continues to Grow   174

Bibliography   177
Index   187
About the Author   191

Acknowledgements

I could not have written this book without help and encouragement from so many people.

Thank you to all those I interviewed formally or informally: Amelia Yancey Bond, Dave Brown, Richard Coadwell, Connie Hubbard Corn, Marielle DeJong, Bob Delwiche, John and Joan Dickson, Stuart English, Forest Supervisor Susan Fay, Marilyn and Kit Garren, William Graham, Marty Griffin, Forest Supervisor Jason Guidry, Gwen Hill, Alan Hirsch, Chan Hubbard, Diane Jacober, Jeff Jennings, Earle Johnson, Ashok Kudva, Sara Landry, Ellen McCotter, Chuck McGrady, Chet Meinzer, Mac Morrow, Barbara Johnson Orr, Jim Parham, Chuck Ramsey, Al Richie, Kieran Roe, Skip (Arnold) Shelton, Aleen Steinberg, Bill Thomas, Jamie Van Buskirk, Dave Vance, Jay Watson and Jackie West.

Marcy Thompson of the Rowell Bosse North Carolina archives of the Transylvania County Library and Kent Wilcox, History Committee chair of Friends of DuPont Forest, provided valuable information and insight on DuPont Forest's history. The Hagley Library in Wilmington, Delaware, was a great source of information and photographs, as was Katie Breckheimer.

Thank you to Diane Jacqmin, who drew the map for the inside front cover; Tom Lucha, who drove me on challenging roads; Erin Major, who took my author photo; and Linda Spangler, who offered me a flower picture. Neil Bernstein, Marielle DeJong, Barbara Morgan and Steve Pierce were invaluable as beta readers.

Acknowledgements

Thank you to Kate Jenkins, acquisition editor at The History Press, who guided me through the publication with patience and kindness. Thank you also to Katie Parry and Jonny Foster for great marketing work and advice, Ryan Finn and the book production team. The History Press is such a pleasure to work with.

And thank you to Nicole Ayers, my book coach and book confidante—I couldn't have done it without you.

Cast of Major Characters

This is a list of people who shaped DuPont Forest history in a major way.

Anthony, Jim—real estate developer
Brown, Dave—first DuPont Forest supervisor
Cart, Ben—owner of Summit Camps
Coxe, Frank—major landowner before DuPont Corporation
du Pont, E.I. de Nemours—founder of DuPont Corporation
Easley, Mike—attorney general under Governor Jim Hunt
Fay, Susan—forest supervisor, Holmes Educational State Forest
Guidry, Jason—current DuPont Forest supervisor
Guion, Alex—major landowner before DuPont Corporation
Hill, Gwen—equestrian
Hirsch, Alan—former deputy attorney general
Holmes, John Simcox—first North Carolina forester
Hubbard, Chan—DuPont Corporation retiree
Hunt, Jim—North Carolina governor, 1977–85, 1993–2001
Jennings, Jeff—former DuPont Corporation employee and environmental activist
Johnson, Earle—DuPont Corporation retiree
Landry, Sara—executive director of Friends of DuPont Forest
McGrady, Chuck—North Carolina State Representative and environmental activist
Meinzer, Chet—DuPont/Corteva property manager

Cast of Major Characters

Paxton, Charlie—DuPont Corporation forester
Staton, Lewis—DuPont Corporation retiree and activist for Staton Road
Steinberg, Aleen—environmental activist
Thomas, Micajah—settler and owner of Buck Spring Hotel
Van Buskirk, Jamie—DuPont/Corteva environmental engineer
West, Jackie—equestrian

PART I
Exploring the Forest

WHY DUPONT FOREST?

How did an industrial site become a forest attracting hikers, equestrians and mountain bikers from all over the United States? This story is about Southern Appalachian grit and self-reliance, a multinational company's generosity, local activists and, of course, a forest, now protecting thousands of acres of trees, lakes and waterfalls.

The first hike I took in DuPont Forest was to High Falls. Like other visitors, I gawked and stared at the falls as I clicked one shot after another. It was a spectacular waterfall. Then I turned around and spotted a tall chimney on a hill. I walked up the wooden steps and saw that the chimney had a fireplace on two sides. A date had been engraved in the concrete. No other clue, no plaque, no sign—I was not in a museum. But I knew there was a story here beyond the waterfalls.

I fell in love with DuPont Forest on that first hike when I visited only a few years after its creation. If the six iconic waterfalls in DuPont State Recreational Forest were more difficult to reach, if they involved a long backpack, they would be featured in *National Geographic* magazine. Instead, Western North Carolina is so lucky to have this forest in its backyard with easy, accessible trails.

Most trails are multi-use. I am a hiker, and I like my feet firmly on the ground. I quickly learned to share the trails with mountain bikers, equestrians, dog lovers, strollers, trail runners and a few North Carolina Forest Service trucks. Several wide trails were created as roads and are driven by forest service staff and volunteers.

Before I plunge into the forest's multilayered history, I need to summarize what the main attractions are now: six waterfalls, five lakes, several mountains, more than one hundred miles of trails and many artifacts that were built before the land became a state forest: a large chimney, an airstrip, a barbecue pit in the most unusual place, a gazebo on a lake, a covered bridge, fancy stone pillars at several forest entrances and more. Each waterfall has its own beauty, its own rhythm, its own admirers. More than twelve thousand acres make up the recreational state forest, the first and only one in North Carolina. This means that the forest strives to encourage recreation while still facilitating some hunting, logging and other accepted forest activities.

DuPont Forest is not untouched wilderness. The terrain in Southern Appalachia has been lived on, tilled, grazed, lumbered and burned. Western North Carolina and Eastern Tennessee are blessed with an abundance of public land. By the time George Vanderbilt, one of many heirs to the Commodore Cornelius Vanderbilt fortune, died in 1914, he had amassed 125,000 acres of land. His widow, Edith, sold over half of the acreage to the U.S. Forest Service at bargain prices, creating Pisgah National Forest. Farther west, Great Smoky Mountains National Park was created from land bought from logging companies and small farmers. Every piece of public land in the Southern Appalachians has a human history—some more obvious than others.

But DuPont Forest's history is still unfolding in the news, maps and trails right now. Even the name tells us that the multinational company had and still has a major part to play in the future of the forest; yes, *that* DuPont, "Better Living through Chemistry" DuPont—E.I. du Pont de Nemours, headquartered in Wilmington, Delaware. What can we learn about industry's role in saving land and making it public?

When I was a newcomer to the area, I asked about the history from fellow hikers. I got bits and pieces of information based on folklore and hearsay. The facts differed based on how long my companions had been in the area. Everyone had a different opinion on the forest's past. So I decided to dig into it myself. I got facts and recollections from many sources and tried to fit together the jigsaw puzzle that is DuPont Forest history. I searched for a book on the DuPont Forest story. While there must be hundreds of books on Great Smoky Mountains National Park and several on the Blue Ridge Parkway, none has been published on this forest. How was that possible? I

Exploring the Forest

Vaporizer boilers at the DuPont plant, 1974. *Courtesy of the Rowell Bosse North Carolina Room, Transylvania County Library.*

spent two years talking to people from all aspects of DuPont Forest, past and present: DuPont Corporation retirees, North Carolina legislators, North Carolina State Forest rangers, conservation leaders, natives, Friends of DuPont activists and forest users. I was determined to put the story together.

First, I talked to DuPont engineers and chemists. They were a pleasure to interview: punctual at our meetings, exact with their words and making sure that I understood them. No one said, "Oh it's too technical." When they could not remember or could not be precise, they said so. I let them talk and tell me their stories. They appeared pleased to educate me.

Years ago, when I told my parents that I was going to marry an engineer, my dad was thrilled. "Engineers make the best husbands," he said, which at the time seemed absurd. But overall, engineers are smart, dedicated to their job, make a good salary and are too busy or indifferent to cheat. These are good odds for a successful marriage and a happy life. These are also good odds for a successful interview.

Over the years, I had hiked many trails in DuPont Forest, some over and over again. But when I decided to write about the forest, I created a spreadsheet of all the trails and hiked methodically through this list, trying to understand the connections between trails. Even the trail names offer a big clue that there is a long human history: Cart, Guion, Joanna, Micajah, Moore…who were all these people?

If we believe that we only care about places that we've seen and experienced, then DuPont Forest should be well loved. Visitors have increased year after year. Waterfalls, lakes, mountain biking and scenes from famous movies have all contributed to DuPont Forest's appeal.

This written portrait of DuPont Forest uses historic documents, DuPont Corporation memos, newsletters, Friends of DuPont research and photographs, North Carolina Forest Service reports and newspaper clippings. But it is a memoir of the forest because it also relies on the best recollections of people in the area at various times. I have interviewed DuPont retirees and former employees, children of retirees, forest service leaders, activists, Transylvania County natives and residents. I looked to them not to necessarily remember dates but to relate incidents, relationships and analysis. *DuPont Forest: A History* blends descriptions of the past and present punctuated by interviews and hiking narratives. Enjoy the book, but more important, get out and enjoy the forest.

RECALLING A BUCK FOREST CHILDHOOD

It's no surprise that adults and children remember their stay at Buck Forest Lodge differently. Buck Forest Hunt Club was a fishing and hunting club organized in the High Falls area; the lodge was built in 1941. Its members brought their families to enjoy just being outdoors. Frank Coxe, James and Dorothy Stikeleather and the Yancey family owned more than five thousand acres. The club lasted until 1956, when DuPont Corporation bought its land.

"The children spent all their time outdoors," Ellen McCotter remembers in a recent discussion. "We'd play at High Falls all day, hiking and sliding down a tributary of the falls. After two or three trips down the falls, our jeans were ripped, but so what? Maybe we got back to the lodge for a sandwich when we were hungry."

McCotter was part of a group from Marion, North Carolina, that visited Buck Forest Lodge from the time she was a young child until she was fifteen years old, when the club folded. Most of her memories are from the early 1950s.

Exploring the Forest

Buck Forest Lodge. *Courtesy of Friends of DuPont Forest.*

Joshua Camblos, eighty-eight years old when interviewed in 2005, remembers that "you had to be twelve years old to fish, and all children and teenagers needed to be with an adult if they fished or went into the woods, as it was considered a dangerous place." Camblos, a physician, was in his thirties when he stayed at Buck Forest and probably already a parent. "The children always wanted to cross the river above the falls which was forbidden and dangerous," he adds.

McCotter now agrees that crossing above High Falls was risky. "When we children went across High Falls, we would form a human chain—just held hands—so that everyone would get across the falls safely and no one would be left on the other side."

Sam Yancey, one of the landowners, brought his family and friends from Marion to Buck Forest frequently; they often had as many as twenty people. His daughter, Amelia Yancey Bond, who was best friends with McCotter, still calls Buck Forest her happy place. The Yancey family brought Ellen and her family as frequent guests. Margaret, their maid, came to cook for this large contingent.

The adults had extended cocktail parties on a rock in front of High Falls using the water from the falls to mix their drinks. It seems like it was a happy place for parents as well. A picture of the Marion gang shows a group of blond children in shorts and women in casual dresses and flat shoes.

Buck Forest Lodge, interior. *Courtesy of Friends of DuPont Forest.*

Al Richie, also a young member of the Marion gang, ran around with the boys. They always tried to find new places to go. "After breakfast, they turned us loose. We were cautioned every day about staying away from the top of the waterfall," Richie says. "In the evening, the adults wanted to get rid of the kids and play cards. And we were worn out."

"The girls were too slow," Richie says. "They would be behind us and we tried to lose them. We never saw any wildlife. A bear or deer would have heard us coming from a mile away. My dad spent the day fly fishing. The river was very close to the lodge."

Exploring the Forest

One day, the boys found a dead snake close to Buck Forest Lodge. As a prank, they curled it up and put it on the doorstep as they were leaving to go back home. When the next group of visitors came to the lodge, a woman walked up to the door, carrying food and dishes in her arms, saw the snake, dropped everything and ran back to her car.

Both Ellen McCotter's and Al Richie's fathers were executives at a mill in Marion. "We were all Episcopalians," McCotter recalls. "The Yanceys took us for a long weekend. From Friday afternoon when the men got off work to Sunday afternoon." The lodge was reserved for the Yanceys and friends; it was just their group. Each family also had two weeks per year at the lodge with unlimited hunting and fishing. It was akin to a timeshare.

Big Sam, as Sam Yancey Sr. was known, came from an old family in McDowell County and owned a lot of land in the county. Sam knew the falls and the paths of the Buck Forest area and was able to lead others to Hooker and Bridal Veil Falls.

Adults played bridge and helped Margaret cook. All the shopping had been done before they came. They brought coolers, ice, everything. Once they were at the lodge, they didn't leave the forest. "Sometimes the fridge would work. Sometimes it didn't," Richie says.

Amelia Bond remembers sleeping in a dormitory-style room with other girls on the ground floor. "There were cots and bunk beds set up. The boys

Crossing above High Falls by car. *Courtesy of the Rowell Bosse North Carolina Room, Transylvania County Library.*

were in a room upstairs. The lodge had a wraparound porch. Daddy set up target shooting from the porch."

The lodge had running water with a pump that had to be primed. "I had to go down the hill, find the pump and prime it. You primed it by putting water on the top and that got it going. Then I hit it to start the pumping. My father gave me twenty-five cents each time I did this. That's how we got water in the bathrooms and kitchen. We had flush toilets, though we had to wait for the tank to fill," Bond recalls. "Wasn't that amazing?"

Bill Duckworth, a real estate appraiser interviewed in 2001, recalls that "the lodge didn't have electricity. We used gas and oil lamps." He emphasizes that the club wasn't just about hunting. "It was fishing, swimming and also fellowship."

Frank Coxe, whose ancestors first came to the North American colonies in the early 1700s, was the majority owner of the Buck Forest property. Duckworth remembers that Coxe related to fellow lodge members a conversation with a DuPont Company representative who came down to look at the property. "He said that it was the purest water he'd ever seen. The purest air he'd ever seen. And when he said that, I figured you'uns lost your place." And that's what happened.

When the DuPont Corporation bought the property, it removed most of the lodge right away. "I'm surprised that DuPont didn't refurbish the lodge to entertain corporate guests," Bill Duckworth says. All that remains of Buck Forest Lodge is the chimney by the High Falls picnic shelter with its fading inscription, a wonderful view of High Falls…and memories.

WHAT IS IN DUPONT FOREST TODAY

To understand how DuPont Forest came to be, it's useful to see what attractions the forest offers the visitor right now. The forest lies between Hendersonville and Brevard, North Carolina; Cedar Mountain is the closest community. The big cities, big being relative, are Asheville, North Carolina, to the north and Greenville, South Carolina, to the south.

As of winter 2020, the forest was 12,239 acres, ranging in altitude from 2,240 feet below Hooker Falls at Cascade Lake to 3,620 feet at the top of Stone Mountain. DuPont Forest, part of the "Land of Waterfalls," has steep slopes and hard rock that does not erode, creating the right conditions for waterfalls. Is there anyone who doesn't love waterfalls? The sound of rushing water, the rocks that remain covered by water or poke out during a drought. The water level is different every time you visit. The wind blows the water a unique way, shifting the flow. Sometimes the air is still. Rhododendrons and mountain laurel framing the rocks change the perception of the scene.

DuPont Forest has six waterfalls, and this is what most visitors come to see: High Falls, Triple Falls, Hooker Falls, Bridal Veil, Wintergreen and Grassy Creek, which is more of a cascade. What is the difference between a waterfall and a cascade? A cascade remains in contact with the underlying rock. A waterfall flows over a lip and over the edge of a cliff—picture Niagara Falls.

Hooker Falls has a vertical drop of about fourteen feet, forming a C-shaped ledge. With so much water falling in a short distance, it gives off the distinctive waterfall roar. Some people swim in the pool formed by the waterfall, although the water is cold even in the height of summer.

High Falls is about one hundred feet. In many places, the slope of the rock face is so gentle that water cascades down the rock and then plunges down to the bottom. A trail leads to the base of the falls. Because you can safely get close, you notice how the falls change each time you visit.

Triple Falls has three levels totaling one hundred feet. The three levels are best seen and photographed from the trail. To get closer, but not that close, a wooden staircase leads to a spot between the lower falls and the two higher falls.

Bridal Veil Falls, with a total drop over one hundred feet, spreads out like a curtain of water. From a wooden platform on the trail, a second, higher drop is visible. Getting closer to the bottom of the falls, only one level can be seen. But that's the photo you see everywhere; each picture looks different, depending on the water level or the angle of the photographs. It looks like the water doesn't know which way to go.

The four waterfalls above are on the Little River, while the next two are on Grassy Creek. Wintergreen Falls is only twenty feet of shooting water. It requires some rock scrambling off Wintergreen Falls Trail. Since it's a little more secluded, the waterfall has an intimate, friendly feel—though perhaps not as spectacular as the others.

Grassy Creek Falls is reached easily from its top. The drop is so slight that it might look like a cascading river. There's a flat outcrop for a side view of the swirling water. The access to the bottom of the waterfall is closed.

The waterfalls have been here since the beginning of time, but the five lakes in DuPont Forest were constructed in the second half of the twentieth century. Western North Carolina has no natural lakes because it was never

Mountain bikers pumping up a hill. *Author's collection.*

subject to glaciers and glacier retreat. In the South, lakes were built for a variety of reasons: power generation, flood control or recreation. On the DuPont property, Lakes Julia, Fawn, Dense, Alford and Imaging were created for swimming, boating, fishing and just sitting and relaxing. Like the waterfalls, each has its charm and own character. They should be explored in all four seasons.

Six access areas (as parking lots are called here) around the forest lead to a hundred miles of trails. Visitors park on the fringe of the forest and not in front of waterfalls and other attractions. You have to walk, mountain bike or get on a horse to reach the attractions; all trails are multi-use.

Every year, a few people fall from waterfalls in the "Land of Waterfalls." Unfortunately for some, it's fatal. Waterfalls are not dangerous. As Kevin Adams, the eminent waterfall photographer, wrote in his book, *North Carolina Waterfalls*, "Waterfalls don't reach out and grab people and fling them over the top." It's people who put themselves in danger by getting too close to the water, climbing to the top of waterfalls or bushwhacking around the sides. Many visitors wear sandals or street shoes, thinking, "Oh I'm not going very far." But close to slippery rocks, moss and roots on the trail, you need boots or at the very least heavy-duty sneakers and hiking socks.

PART II
Settlers and Land Barons

MEETING THE FIRST SETTLERS

Breathes there the man with soul so dead
Who never to himself hath said,
This is my own, my native land!
—Sir Walter Scott (1771–1832)

Although Sir Walter Scott never came to Western North Carolina, he got the sentiment correct. He would have felt right at home in the Cedar Mountain area. As Scott was growing up, the American Revolution was raging. The nearest Revolutionary War activity here occurred in Waynesville, fifty miles northwest of Cedar Mountain.

During the Revolutionary War, the Continental Congress promised bounty land as an inducement to military service. The first family deed was offered to John Thomas Jr. as a land grant. The deed was registered in 1799 from Buncombe County; at the time, everything west of Asheville was part of Buncombe County. The land included the "three lower falls," which most probably were High Falls, Triple Falls and Bridal Veil Falls. It must have been considered good land. Although the area was isolated, with rocky terrain in places, it had plenty of water.

At the same time that John Thomas was granted land, E.I. du Pont de Nemours was on a ship from France to the East Coast of the United

DuPont Forest

Crossing at High Falls by horse and carriage. *Courtesy of the Rowell Bosse North Carolina Room, Transylvania County Library.*

States. He and his extended family left the chaos of the aftermath of the French Revolution. Two years later, du Pont started his gunpowder company in Wilmington, Delaware. By now, Tench Coxe owned plenty of land in "Carolana," though at this point not in the Cedar Mountain area. He had inherited and bought more land, dubbed the "Speculation Lands."

The Cedar Mountain area was in a disputed part of North Carolina and Georgia. Between 1804 and 1811, the two states quarreled about which owned a twelve-mile strip of land dubbed "the orphan strip." While it was orphan territory falling between two states, the area was ruled by outlaws and ruffians. Then Georgia claimed it and named the area Walton County after George Walton, one of three signers of the Declaration of Independence from that state. Georgia tried to collect taxes from area residents, without much success.

The area went from orphan status to being claimed by both North Carolina and Georgia. Several skirmishes ensued. A joint commission studied the problem and gave the piece to North Carolina. But Georgia wasn't satisfied. The state line was supposed to be the 35th parallel, but where was that? The State of Georgia hired Andrew Ellicott, a noted surveyor from Pennsylvania, to find the line. He and his men bushwhacked through rhododendron and mountain laurel and established that the orphan strip belonged to North Carolina—an orphan no more. Now the disputed land is part of Transylvania County.

Settlers and Land Barons

Micajah Thomas, one of John Thomas's three sons, was born in 1808. Micajah (the name is of Hebrew origin and means "who is like God?") lived and farmed the Cedar Mountain area. A trail in the Corn Mill Shoals section of DuPont Forest is named after him. In 1813, after the Walton skirmish, John Thomas Jr. parceled his land to his three sons. Robert Thomas, one of the sons, later became the first sheriff of Henderson County.

Micajah Thomas, who had twelve children, stayed in the area and became the family leader in Corn Mill Shoals. Joanna Mountain was named after his daughter. In the early 1850s, Micajah built Buck Forest Hotel at the intersection of present-day Cascade Road and Staton Road, which was a stagecoach stop. The hotel entertained guests who were traveling from Upstate South Carolina to the cooler climate of the North Carolina mountains. Thomas was quite an entrepreneur and builder; he also opened the Cedar Mountain Post Office at the hotel.

But guests needed to be able to reach Buck Forest Hotel in the mountains. This was the age of the turnpikes. The Buncombe Turnpike, which took travelers from the South Carolina border through North Carolina to the Tennessee border, was built between 1824 and 1828. It's credited with encouraging people to settle in Western North Carolina. In the Brevard area, visitors came up the Jones Gap Turnpike.

Solomon Jones, a local legend, was a self-taught road builder. According to folklore, Jones set a sow free to blaze a trail, which he then followed with a

Buck Forest Hotel. *Courtesy of the Rowell Bosse North Carolina Room, Transylvania County Library.*

hatchet. In the 1840s, he created a path known as the Jones Gap Toll Road from Cedar Mountain to Greenville. The toll road, which Jones charged to access, brought tourists to the mountains. In the 1930s, US 276 opened, making for much easier travel down to Upstate South Carolina. Now the old toll road is part of Jones Gap State Park. Two other turnpikes converged here to make Buck Forest Hotel an attractive proposition.

The mountains did not spare residents from the ravages of the Civil War. Micajah was blinded in one eye during an attack. After the Civil War, he sold the hotel to Joseph Carson. Carson's brother-in-law, Colonel Franklin Coxe, paid for the hotel and retained the title. That may have been the origin of the Frank Coxe family's large Buck Forest holdings. Carson continued to operate the hotel until the early 1900s. By then, the hotel was falling apart and no longer on the main route to the mountains.

With all the water available, it's not surprising that enterprising settlers built mills around waterfalls. In 1882, three brothers—Spencer, Edmund and John Hooker—purchased land and a gristmill from Clinton Moore around the falls that bear their names. John stayed in the area, while the other brothers went to South Carolina. Later, in 1910, his land and all the mill equipment were sold to Tench Charles Coxe.

Clinton Moore is buried at the Hooker-Moore Cemetery, located close to Hooker Falls. The cemetery once served Laurel Creek Baptist Church, but now Cascade Lake covers the church site. Official records may have disappeared, but there are no Hookers in the Hooker-Moore Cemetery. The name might come from the cemetery's proximity to Hooker Falls. There are about sixty-five graves in the cemetery, but only a few graves are legible.

Isaac Heath and his family lived in the DuPont Forest area through the Civil War. Descendants of the Isaac Heath family have placed new tombstones identifying the graves, which helps to piece together the lives of some of those buried here. The most heartbreaking is the story of the 1861 epidemic when Isaac Heath lost four of his ten children, probably to diphtheria. He personally buried them, as he did not want others to contract the disease. The land was heavily logged. Little by little, residents all sold their property to larger landowners who consolidated their holdings.

Thomas Cemetery, the other named graveyard, can be reached from the Guion Farm Access Area. While the Hooker-Moore Cemetery was a community cemetery where several families are buried, the Thomas Cemetery holds only the Thomas families.

"Here, the graves are buried by date, the oldest being in the top right corner," says Patty Stahl, a volunteer guide at DuPont Forest. "This is

Isaac Heath grave at Hooker-Moore Cemetery. *Author's collection.*

certainly something I never would have figured out, even with all the times I've been here."

The oldest grave is of a toddler, Thomas M. Thomas, grandson of Micajah Thomas. Micajah died in 1883 and is grave number three in Thomas Cemetery. Stahl, a descendant of Isaac Heath, has documented all these graves. The tallest stone isn't a grave marker but rather a memorial with several engraved names and dates. Most graves are buried under moss-covered rocks without much identification.

VISITING THE LAND OF THE SKY

Christian Reid was the pen name of Mrs. Frances Christine Fisher Tiernan (1846–1920). Although she was a prolific novelist, her best-known book is *The Land of the Sky: Adventures in Mountain By-Ways*, her tenth novel, which was published in 1876. The novel is illustrated with black-and-white sketches. Women are shown in long dresses, hats and fans. Tiernan, the daughter of a railroad official in Salisbury, North Carolina, was considered a low lander.

And like others who could afford it, she and her friends looked to get out of the heat every summer.

In this story, a group of young unencumbered men and women choose to travel through the mountains of Western North Carolina. But a great nature lover advises against it. "You will find no fashionable hotels, no bands of music…." Still, they go looking for diversions. The men might hunt and fish, while the women could admire the beauty of the area.

Trains had not yet arrived in the area, so they traveled in carriages, which was a scary proposition. Tiernan describes the road as a mere shelf. When they have to pass another vehicle, Tiernan imagines being pushed over a precipice and hitting rocks and rushing water below.

The group eventually finds its way to Buck Forest and the hotel. The hotel is depicted as a "large two-story building, with a long piazza in front." Antlers and hunting horns decorate the walls, and "long-eared, soft-eyed hounds" lie about the room. There are shade trees and mountains close by. Dinner, probably the midday meal in those days, features a piece of tender, well-dressed venison.

Buck Forest Hotel is a place for sportsmen. The men in the group find the owner an ideal mountain host. But what could women do at the hotel to amuse themselves? As predicted, the ladies have been warned that they won't like the hotel or setting. "No mineral waters to drink, no grounds to lounge over." But they find plenty to do.

The group explores Castle Rock, a cliff off current US 276 in the community of Dunns Rock. The women are not deterred by their long skirts, hats and flimsy shoes from climbing up the slope. Later, they find Rich Mountain; unlike today, there was no road to the top.

But some things never change. At Bridal Veil Falls, a woman in the group gets too close to the water and falls in but insists she's not hurt. They admire High Falls and Triple Falls. After a week, they decide to move on to Caesar's Head, in Upstate South Carolina.

Tiernan is dismissed in serious literary circles as a "colorist," a term used for women novelists who emphasize peculiarities of quaint locals. However, Tiernan did much to raise awareness of the beauty of the Southern Appalachian Mountains. The phrase "Land of the Sky" became the popular slogan for Western North Carolina and Asheville in particular. It brought in tourists and still does. "Land of the Sky" is used by realtors, tourist bureaus and churches.

George Taylor, a traveler who came through the same area on a wagon trip from Greenville in 1877, may have been influenced by the Tiernan books.

He writes that he enjoyed his trips to Caesar's Head, Cedar Mountain and the Buck Forest Hotel, where he commented favorably on the scenery and company. Travelers such as Taylor continued to visit the area, and Cedar Mountain was the site of the major tourist development at this time, being the closest point in the mountains to Greenville and Spartanburg, South Carolina.

By 1894, the atmosphere at Buck Forest Hotel had changed. John D. Muller, a young man traveling to the Upstate, writes a four-page letter to his mother in Charleston describing his journey. He and his companion, whom he refers to as "the professor," took the train to Hendersonville, North Carolina, and planned to walk to Caesar's Head. They know that they will find a fine hotel once they get to their destination. On the way, they look for lodging. Unlike modern hikers, they are not planning to camp. On the second day, they find Buck Forest Hotel. As Muller describes it:

> *By 5 p.m. we reached a rather forlorn looking building, ornamented with many antlers of various deer which had been killed during the past forty or fifty years. These antlers gave the name to the place—"Buck Forest Hotel." The proprietor no longer bothers himself about possible guests. He tried to put us off and send us a mile further to Squire Heath's, but—we used a little persuasion and so obtained a bed. He had nothing to eat in the house so our supper that night and first meal the next morning consisted of crackers we had brought along and milk from the hotel cow. The milk was a redeeming feature. Oh, it was so rich and sweet and cool. He had put the milk bottle in a spring to cool. Somebody gave the man a Jersey cow some time ago, so we had jersey milk. His name is Carson, and he is a distant relative of the famous frontiersman, Indian scout, trapper & hunter, Kit Carson.*

By 7:30 a.m., the two men are off again. Once they arrive at Caesar's Head hotel, they take a bath and rest before dinner at 2:00 p.m.:

> *We are having a splendid time: going by slow stages and poking into every hole and corner to see the wonders & beauties hidden away from the busy world by nature. I guess you will have to come up too next month and breathe this pure mountain air and lead this simple, unostentatious life. What do you say?*

Even in those days, young men could not depend on their youth and vigor to keep them fit. In a postscript, he writes, "[B]oth well but the Prof feels stiff and sore. My training in the YMCA gym helps me…in good condition."

KINGDOM OF THE HAPPY LAND

The story of the settlers in Cedar Mountain is not just the story of White Anglo-Saxons moving into the area. A community of African Americans settled in the Tuxedo area and gave itself the name the "Kingdom of the Happy Land." The story of how they got here is told by Sadie Smathers Patton, a local Henderson County historian, through an eighteen-page booklet published in 1957.

After the Civil War, the South was devastated, and its plantations were ruined. Newly freed people were no longer a source of wealth—now they were a liability. Where would African Americans go? Many moved off the land of their former homes and wandered about. In Mississippi, William Montgomery became the leader of a small group of followers heading north. Patton describes him as a "man of light color." His father was a "white plantation master" and his mother "a young Negro woman." He was a house servant who had learned to read and write.

The leader and his freed people headed north. They recruited as they went along, like the Pied Piper without the tragic ending. In South Carolina, they heard that before the war White folks had gone to the mountains to get away from the heat. People from the Lowcountry who could afford it owned houses in Western North Carolina long before the Civil War. Montgomery's traveling pilgrims pictured mountains stretching for miles; maybe they could find some land. To the caravan of former slaves looking for a place to settle, this must have sounded like the land of milk and honey.

By then, the group size could have been anywhere from fifty to two hundred people. They arrived at the home of Colonel John Davis, by then deceased. His wife, Miss Serepta Merritt Davis, and their son, Tom, no longer had anyone to tend their land. Patton's small book describes the negotiations between Miss Serepta and Montgomery, the leader of the pilgrims. The group moved into cabins that had been previously occupied by enslaved people and were now standing empty. They agreed to do the fieldwork necessary to make the land productive again and earn their keep on the farm. They planted gardens and fed chickens; women cooked in the kitchen.

Patton describes the kingdom "in a small valley with people living on surrounding hills." It sounds like Camelot. "Farm tilled by people of the Happy Land produced an abundance to spare," Patton writes. The land was located on a stagecoach route where travelers sought food and lodging.

The residents also made and sold Happy Land liniment, which was known to be good for rheumatism and aching muscles and bones. Revenues from all the enterprise went into the communal pot, where it was managed by the King, as William Montgomery was known.

In the early 1870s, the original leader who brought people to the mountains died. Robert Montgomery—some accounts identify him as the brother of William—became the new King in 1872. His sister-in-law, Louella Montgomery, was the Queen. For a while, the Kingdom became more prosperous. However, when the railroad came in and passed near the Kingdom in 1878, this was the beginning of the end. Stagecoach travel ceased, and so did the need for stagecoach stops; train travel was faster and more comfortable.

The Kingdom bought land from heirs of the Davises in 1882. Seven years later, the land was sold to pay taxes after Robert Montgomery died. The residents started looking for work in nearby towns. People moved away. Women found jobs in White households. Jerry Casey, the last remaining member of the colony, died in 1918. This community lasted from 1864 to 1900.

There were rumors that the Black pilgrims had brought gold coins to the Happy Land and hid them between stones in the cabins. Joseph Bell, who purchased the land, built Lake Summit and founded the Green River Manufacturing Company. Later, the family established camps around the lake. The family owns the land to this day, although seventy-five acres on the South Carolina side were sold under eminent domain for the Greenville watershed. But no gold was ever found.

Sadie Smathers Patton's booklet is a treasure found in the reference section of local libraries. It includes a hand-drawn map of the location of the Kingdom, shown to the east of Lake Summit in Tuxedo, off US 225. Patton's main source of information was Reverend Ezel Couch, then eighty-five years old, who was brought to the Kingdom at one year of age. Patton studied law and became a court reporter, serving most of the Western North Carolina counties. She's best known for *The Story of Henderson County*, which is still considered the definitive history.

FINDING CHEROKEE PETROGLYPHS

The Friends of DuPont Forest offers lectures and walks for its members as a way to encourage people to join the Friends group and support the forest. On his Cherokee Lecture and Walk, Dr. Keith Parker discusses the early Cherokees in the Cedar Mountain area and takes us on a short walk to see nearby petroglyphs.

We know that there were European settlers in what is now DuPont Forest from the 1700s. Two cemeteries hold the remains of inhabitants in the area. Other artifacts remind us of DuPont Forest's history before it became a state forest. So it's no surprise that Cherokees lived and passed through the area long before that.

The Cherokees left us petroglyphs, pictures that were dug and scratched in rocks but not painted. Today, Parker lectures on petroglyphs in the classroom behind the Visitor Center. Most of the audience members live locally and know one another. I may have come the farthest, all the way from Asheville.

According to Parker, no one knows what the petroglyphs mean. The scratches can take on four fundamental symbols: circle, square, center and cross. In DuPont Forest, circles prevail. Some believe that petroglyphs are a sign from outer space, but I just let that theory wash over me; the Cherokee connection is more relevant. Dr. Parker quotes Forest Service Archaeologist Scott Ashcroft, "There are more sites of ancient peoples uncovered by archaeological excavations in Transylvania County than any other place in the state."

Parker spends a lot of time talking about Judaculla Rock in Jackson County, about sixty miles west of the forest. The large boulder is covered in etchings, probably done between 3000 and 1000 BCE, and considered a sacred site for the Cherokee Nation. Judaculla, a one-eye giant, sat in judgment over those who hunted game on what has come to be known as the Devil's Courthouse of the Blue Ridge Parkway. After years of abuse and neglect, Judaculla Rock is now protected. Parker gives us driving instructions on how to find it.

Then we all leave the classroom and drive to Corn Mill Shoals access area, about a ten- to fifteen-minute drive from the Visitor Center. We hike up Big Rock Trail, a trail rutted by a lot of bike traffic. When I hiked Big Rock Trail a few weeks prior, I noticed the big rocks but did not pay attention to the petroglyphs.

Asked specifically about what is known regarding these circular petroglyphs in DuPont Forest, Parker is very direct: "We just don't know." The circle is a common universal symbol for many things with social and mythical meanings. It can mean motion, perfection, no end, no beginning, sun, moon, protection, inclusion, exclusion, celestial cycles, animal cycles, night, day and movement of time. Other possible representations could be the feminine gender and a magical boundary not to be crossed. In Jungian theory, the circle is the archetypal symbol of our totality—what we are.

But to see the large group of petroglyphs, you need to get off the trail. A short path to the right takes us to a large expanse of rocks. The group starts looking down. You don't have to be an archaeologist to see these scratched circles—lots and lots of them.

The photos I take give the impression that they've been shot in black-and-white, but no—that's what the rock looks like. The twenty or so hikers spread out and call out their finds. We each seem to find our own favorite petroglyphs as we traverse the rock.

In the recent past, Big Rock Trail went right over these petroglyphs. But members of Friends of DuPont who knew about these Cherokee treasures asked for the trail to be moved. They were rightly concerned that the constant biking would wear away the petroglyphs. Finally, the North Carolina Forest Service agreed. Sometimes it just pays to get off the beaten path.

GROWING UP IN CEDAR MOUNTAIN

Before World War II, life was not easy in the community of Cedar Mountain. Even John Snyder, a White boy from a relatively comfortable family, always seemed to be troubled, cold and scared. He dreamed that panthers and snakes would come in his back bedroom. It was 1938, and John Snyder, the author, was four years old.

"In winter it is so cold," John Snyder writes in his memoir, *Hill of Beans: Coming of Age in the Last Days of the Old South*, "our breath comes out like white smoke." When the wind blows hard, he could hear trees thrashing and groaning around him. And the whippings from his father! Snyder was the second of four boys in the family, and they were always getting into trouble for something.

Snyder's father, Ted, was a successful contractor who built vacation homes for summer people traveling from Upstate South Carolina. The father married late in life to a much younger woman, and he relished his peace and quiet when he got home from work. After his supper, he liked to listen to the radio. Even with all the static from the radio, he felt, correctly, that another war was brewing in Europe.

At the time, the community of Cedar Mountain was just a store with a post office inside and a few summer houses. Once the Snyders left their unpaved road, they could go into Brevard to do grocery shopping, or "rations," as they called it. The author's mother was very sociable, always cleaning and dusting in case company came. Before telephones, people just showed up. Her family and friends would come up the mountain from Greenville on weekends. In Cedar Mountain, visitors were the lifeline to what was going on outside their community.

At Christmastime, the family went off the mountain to visit the father's family in Greenville. The six of them squeezed in a 1935 Ford to take the twisty road south. Close to the South Carolina line, the old Jones Gap Turnpike had been the old alternative to getting people down the mountain. But they traveled to Greenville on the Geer Highway, now called US 276. John Snyder loved the excitement of Greenville, with its floats in the Christmas parade, the stores and visiting with Santa. But he could not predict he was going to live in Greenville for a few years.

When it was time to send little John to school, just like today's parents, his mother was concerned about the quality of his son's education. The only local option was the one-room Connestee school, but that was not acceptable to his mother. She had been educated as a teacher and encouraged her boys to read and write before they had to attend school.

"I've heard those teachers talk, and they use double negatives," Snyder's mom said. The two oldest boys were sent to live with their two unmarried aunts in Greenville. They attended a city elementary school

The McGaha Chapel in Cedar Mountain is in the National Register of Historic Places. *Author's collection.*

deemed superior to the one in Cedar Mountain. It was a dreary existence punctuated by their aunts' eccentric behavior. Bess, the older and more obstinate one, carried an automatic pistol. When she thought she heard people in the garden at night, she would go to a window and shoot off a few rounds at random into the yard.

John's happiest time as a young child seemed to be with his nanny, Celia McGaha. Celia's father, Joe McGaha, farmed part of the Snyder land. McGaha is still now a prominent name in the Cedar Mountain area. The McGaha family arrived in the area just after 1800, originally from Ireland. The McGaha Chapel, built in 1872, is located in Cedar Mountain on what was the Johnstone Turnpike, a turnpike also superseded by US 276.

The chapel is a tiny one-room building with plain walls and peaked roof. The building rests on stacks of fieldstones. There's no sign or steeple. The chapel thrived until about 1930. When transportation became easier, worshipers went to Brevard for Sunday services. It seemed that the building was forgotten and falling apart. Now the Transylvania County Historical Society owns the chapel. It's open when there are events or by appointment.

What does the title *Hill of Beans* mean? The father would say that the boys wouldn't amount to a hill of beans, but he was wrong. After graduating from the University of Chicago, John Snyder went into the U.S. Navy, became a glass and china buyer and secured several patents for carpet implements, among other accomplishments. His older brother, Ted Snyder, became a lawyer, a renowned environmentalist and national Sierra Club president.

CREATING BUCK FOREST LODGE

Frank Coxe, whose ancestors first came to the North American colonies in the early 1700s, was the majority owner of the Buck Forest property. Joe McD "Uncle Joe" Carson, who ran the dilapidated Buck Forest Hotel into the ground, relinquished the property to Colonel Franklin Coxe of Asheville. The Coxe family, who eventually sold their Buck Forest holdings to the DuPont Corporation, can be traced back to Dr. Daniel Coxe (1640–1730), physician to King Charles II of England. The English doctor bought a great deal of land in the colonies without ever seeing it; he named the area "Carolana." Although he eventually sold it for land in New York, his great-grandson Tench Coxe (1755–1824) became a Pennsylvanian delegate to the Continental Congress. He bought other lands known as "speculative lands" in the Carolinas and coal mines in Pennsylvania. After the Civil War, when the South was struggling, the northern mines saved the family fortune.

Colonel Franklin Coxe, Tench's grandson, moved to Asheville and envisioned the future of the city and the land of the sky. He felt that Western North Carolina was going to be a "tremendous resort area." Once the railroad came to Asheville in 1880, many famous people came to the mountains for rest, a cure and to see the southern mountains.

To capture the tourist market, Colonel Coxe built the Battery Park Hotel in Asheville. The hotel, which opened on July 12, 1886, was set on Battery Park Hill. Built in fanciful Queen Anne style with turrets, towers and gables, it looked like a castle. More importantly, it had an elevator and electric lights, which were novelties in the South. Famous guests included Presidents Grover Cleveland and William McKinley. They were probably happy to get out of Washington, D.C., in the summer and cool off in the mountain air.

Presidents bring cachet to a hotel, and this attracts other guests. George Washington Vanderbilt, one of many grandchildren of Commodore Cornelius Vanderbilt, came here with his mother, Maria Louisa. As the youngest of eight children, he seemed to be the designated caretaker for his mother. She was not in good health, and the mountain air was supposed to cure many ailments. From the veranda of the Battery Park Hotel, Vanderbilt gazed across the valleys and wanted to have his own mountain retreat. Out of this desire, Asheville now has the Biltmore Estate, which to many visitors seems to be the area's main attraction.

By the 1920s, the Battery Park Hotel was getting on in years, and so were the Coxe family owners. When E.W. Grove, a pharmaceutical entrepreneur and self-made millionaire, wanted to buy the hotel, the Coxe family sold it happily. Grove had already built the Grove Park Inn in North Asheville, which attracted its own celebrities. According to a 1979 interview with Frank Coxe, an heir to the Coxe holdings, "He [Grove] wanted to control the hotels in Asheville."

The 1920s were the boom years in Asheville, and nothing seemed too audacious. E.W. Grove was convinced to cut down the hill before he built his new hotel. The new Battery Park Hotel opened in 1924, built of reinforced concrete with straight lines. This hotel lasted until 1972 and now survives as the Battery Park Senior Apartments. In the middle of booming, stylish Asheville, these affordable apartments are in a prime location.

Frank Coxe (1899–1987), grandson of Colonel Franklin Coxe, inherited the Buck Forest land. He grew up in Asheville. Like most boys of his generation and social class, he went to the Asheville School, an elite boarding high school. After Yale and a year in New York City, Coxe returned to Asheville. Frank Coxe became a banker who operated an insurance and real estate business. He was active in civic affairs and served for many years as executive vice-president on the Asheville Industrial Council. This group promoted and encouraged industry to settle in the area.

From Coxe's biography, it seems that the five thousand acres of Buck Forest land owned were a minor part of his family's holdings and investments. He organized the Buck Forest Club in 1941. The club lease covered all the recreational facilities in a tract of land of "approximately five thousand (5,000) acres situated along the waters of Little River, generally known as Buck Forest." The lease, dated February 1, 1941, was for a term of ten years and was to end on January 31, 1951. The first year's rent was $2,000 and then $3,000 per annum thereafter, with an option to renew for an additional five years.

The club lease required the construction of a clubhouse "of rough but substantial construction, to be situated on a suitable site." The construction was to start within the first year and be completed as soon as reasonably possible. The chosen site was on a hill in front of High Falls. The side of the fireplace shows the date as April 28, 1941, and was probably chiseled by Paul F. Roberts, who built the lodge.

The most used part of the lodge must have been the wraparound porch. Pictures of the Marion group taken in 1951 show adults and children on the porch. Today, we might say they were hanging out, talking, walking barefoot on the porch while avoiding the splinters.

Members of the club were young professionals and their families from the Asheville area and points farther east. They must have had some affinity for the outdoors since the lodge did not seem very comfortable, certainly not compared to what they experienced at home. The members also enjoyed socializing with one another.

Photographs taken in the 1930s show three cabins on the property before the lodge was built. All the cabins, along with the clubhouse, were to be available for the exclusive use of club members as they saw fit.

Two small black-and-white photos show Bridal Veil Cabin, built in 1936. The careful hand-lettered caption states that the "Bridal Veil Cabin is completely furnished and has running water already installed. There is an indoor and outdoor fireplace. The interior dimensions are 30X30 with kitchen extension. There is an outside bunkhouse for a servant." The wooden cabin had a large covered porch and a good-sized chimney.

The cabin was located near where the present Bridal Veil Falls Trail starts down to the viewing platform. A dedication party was held for the cabin in

DuPont Forest

Bridal Veil Cabin was to be refurbished by Buck Forest Lodge members. *Courtesy of Friends of DuPont Forest.*

June 1936. The invitees were told to bring a swimsuit if they liked clear, cold water. The travel time from Asheville was noted as two days by foot or two hours by car. The route took guests to Cedar Mountain on the Greenville Highway and then on from there via a rough and unpaved Buck Forest Road.

The Stillwell House between Bridal Veil and High Falls was a "well-built house." From the picture, it looks a lot smaller than the Bridal Veil Cabin. "The plans were to refinish the cabin to be used as an exclusive stag cabin. There are two large rooms downstairs with a large attic dormitory upstairs. A wing to the rear comprises the kitchen." There was no word on whether the cabin was ever remodeled. Amelia Yancey Bond never recalls staying any place but Buck Forest Lodge. "It was much easier to get to High Falls," she said.

The Hooker Cabin at Hooker Falls looks even smaller and more forlorn. The photo caption notes, "As can be readily seen, this house will have to be practically rebuilt. There were high hopes for this cabin…this cabin will be remodeled and outfitted with running water. The location is the lowest of any cabin and is very accessible to the lake area."

It can only be assumed that the reference to running water was to the same prime pumping system that Amelia Bond described and operated for twenty-five cents each time she had to get the water flowing again to Buck Forest Lodge.

As the five lakes were built much later, the lake area that is referred to must be the pool formed by the dam at Hooker Falls. Most of the surrounding land was pasture. Large fields along the river above High Falls and several smaller fields scattered about the remainder of the property were also maintained.

Settlers and Land Barons

Right: Bridal Veil Cabin, another view. *Courtesy of Friends of DuPont Forest.*

Below: On the Buck Forest Lodge porch. *Courtesy of Ellen McCotter.*

It's amazing to think that only one caretaker could manage the whole property. Joe Golden had a house and barn located at the intersection of what is now Joanna Road and Pitch Pine Trail in DuPont Forest. Golden farmed on the property and even had a small sawmill. Buck Forest Lodge members were very concerned with trespassers and poachers—a problem not unique to this parcel of land or this period. Maybe the land was open for hunting before Coxe and his cohorts bought in, or maybe trespassing rules just weren't enforced. Many locals continued to think of Buck Forest as their historic hunting ground.

The club lease specified that a full-time man should be hired to protect the property against fishing, hunting or trespassing by outsiders. While protecting the land from nonmembers, this same man was supposed to "build up the fishing and hunting" for members. On the evening of May 9, 1947, Mother's Day, Joe Golden was found at the bottom of Triple Falls, shot in the chest from his own pistol. No one was ever charged, so the imagination can run overtime. Were they moonshiners or poachers, or was it just a random killing?

HIKE: THREE WATERFALLS IN THREE MILES

I've been hiking in DuPont Forest for years, watching it grow and get more sophisticated over time. Each year, the number of visitors increases. Today, I'm not adventurous; I want to experience the three most popular waterfalls on the Little River as most visitors see them. At 9:30 this morning, the High Falls Access Area is almost empty. Mountain bikers remove their bikes from their car and twiddle with their shoes. I put on my boots and Tilley hat—my uniform.

I start on the High Falls Trail, a path built just for hikers, and then turn on High Falls Loop Trail. Like most wide trails in DuPont Forest, it must have been a road in the past. A stone chimney with a double fireplace, the remnants of Buck Forest Lodge, sits across from the falls. A covered picnic shelter was rehabilitated in 2006 by Friends of DuPont Forest. Mud tubes cling to the ceiling side of the shelter. The organ pipe mud dauber (*Trypoxylon politum*), a predatory wasp, lives here. According to Wikipedia, organ pipe mud daubers are an exceedingly docile species of wasp and generally pleasant to have around, as they serve to keep spider populations down. Really? No wasp is pleasant to have around. I'd rather have the spiders, but today I can't see any creatures around the mud tubes.

The water display flowing down High Falls is dramatic, no matter how much water there actually is. Technically, it's a cascade, falling about one hundred feet. At the top of the falls, a wide covered pedestrian bridge accommodates all users. This bridge was not yet built when the Marion group visited the forest. Some call the bridge an intrusion, but it's just part of DuPont Forest history.

Settlers and Land Barons

"Victoria Falls is the highest falls in the world," a man tells his female companion next to me as we all stare at the flowing water. But he's wrong—Angel Falls in Venezuela are the highest. If we had to expend more time and energy to see the DuPont waterfalls, we would appreciate them a lot more. They'd be featured in a magazine under the heading of "Secrets of the Carolinas." But High Falls is less than a half-mile walk from the parking lot and no mystery.

The view of High Falls is familiar, but a spur trail to the bottom of the falls is a newly signposted trail. It takes me to the base of the falls, where I rock hop around the pool to get as close as I feel comfortable, enjoying the spray. Two visitors fish on a rock almost at the base of the falls. Are they catching anything in this fast-moving water?

I continue to Triple Falls, which also has a picnic shelter. Close by, there's a large round stone table that looks like an old millstone. A round piece of metal is attached to the top like a Lazy Susan, but it does not rotate. Wooden stump seats all around make it perfect for children's birthday parties.

At the top of the staircase leading to the falls, there's a caution sign that has frightened some people. "DANGER Serious injury and death have occurred here"—as if the waterfall was going to reach out and grab you. Still, every year, a few people climb to the top of waterfalls, slip and fall. Sometimes they just break a leg. Other times they plunge to their death. The waterfalls are not inherently dangerous; the water flows to its own rhythm.

A few years ago, I watched as a young well-dressed couple read the sign, took it seriously and walked away without exploring this wonderful spectacle. I wanted to tell them, "Wait, come back. Walk down the stairs. The waterfall is completely safe." But they were taken in by the over-the-top signage and missed what some say is the best waterfall in DuPont Forest.

Danger sign near Triple Falls. *Author's collection.*

A long set of steps built by volunteers from a nearby community college leads to flat rocks between the upper two falls and the lower falls. All together, Triple Falls is about one hundred feet tall. I must have hundreds of photos of these falls, but I take more. Each time I come here, the water level is a little different, so the pictures are different. But the falls always run; they never seem to go dry.

Back on Triple Falls Trail, trailing arbutus hides under rhododendrons. A few patches of purple and halberd-leaved violets cover the forest floors. By now, visitors have started to stream in. A few people climb up the steep trail to Triple Falls, while many linger on rocks lining Little River. I cross the river over a beautiful wooden and metal bridge and head to Hooker Falls.

Hooker Falls is the most accessible of the three falls. There's even a platform for wheelchair visitors. Parents roll strollers down the trail, but they really struggle on the way back up. The wide C-shaped waterfall is only about fourteen feet—not much—but the volume of water is remarkable. It empties into a huge plunge pool. In the summer, the area is like Coney Island. Visitors bring coolers, blankets, folding chairs and dogs. Today, a few people take photos from various vantage points.

Past the "Fishing Access" sign, I follow a social trail up and down. I'm curious where this trail leads, but it really is a fishing access and nothing else. When the rhododendron thicket gets impenetrable, I turn around.

Back at the DuPont Visitor Center, I listen as the volunteer on duty explains to a family that they could visit two waterfalls in two miles or "three for three," as if the waterfalls were on sale. "Go for the three waterfalls," I want to tell them. No other waterfalls are going to be so beautiful and so easy to reach.

On another occasion, I take Ellen McCotter to DuPont Forest so she can share her memories of her Buck Forest childhood on site. She was here as a young teen when the area was still Buck Forest Lodge—place-based history, as they call it. McCotter is a fit and active eighty years old. Our first stop is Hooker Falls. "I know I was here. I wondered how we got here from the lodge," she says. Staton Road had not yet been built, and neither was the bridge. "A couple of adult men led us here. Maybe we just went through the woods."

We then drive to the Visitor Center and walk to the Buck Forest Lodge site. "Yep, here it is," McCotter says.

The chimney has fireplaces on both sides. She surmised that the great room, the living room, was to the right of the chimney as you face the waterfalls and the kitchen to the left. To the right of the living room, there was at least one bedroom with bunk beds. Upstairs there were more bedrooms for adult couples.

On the bridge to Hooker Falls. *Author's collection.*

"The boys slept upstairs as well." McCotter isn't sure but says, "I can't remember how many bathrooms there were. Today, the number of bathrooms in a house would be very important." People entered through the porch, which faced the falls. To the right of the lodge, then and now, is a large flat area. "This must have been where they parked," she said. "We probably came from there," pointing to a small road ahead.

Access roads even then must have been adequate for Frank Coxe, the majority landowner, to be able to sell memberships to the Buck Forest Club. This was the 1940s and 1950s. The type of people attracted to buying a place at the club were not going to walk or use horse and wagon to get to the lodge.

How did the guests drive onto the property from the outside? As a child who didn't drive, McCotter would not have known the roads. Looking at a map, it seems most probable that they drove the Buck Forest Road from the Guion Farm and crossed High Falls at the top. Although the covered bridge would not be built for several decades, the rocks were close enough and water shallow for adventurous cars to caravan and cross.

McCotter and I walk down from the lodge site to the bottom of High Falls on a smooth switch backed trail. "We just headed straight down to the falls when I was a kid. I can't remember if anyone had cut a trail for us." Before the North Carolina Forest Service created a gentle trail to the bottom of High Falls, there was a rough, rocky trail to the right of the falls. The trail was eroded, and the rangers finally closed it. Maybe that was the old trail to which McCotter referred.

We walk down to the bottom of High Falls and take off around the falls. By now, people of all ages are rock hopping, sitting, snacking or splashing around the water. "We didn't have these rocks here," McCotter says. "We

Fording above High Falls by car. *Courtesy of Friends of DuPont Forest.*

must have chosen the shallowest path to the falls and bushwhacked through the island to get to the left there, where the water is a little less rough."

Our next stop is Triple Falls, but McCotter doesn't remember if she was here as a child. On our way back toward the Visitor Center, we take a detour to the covered bridge above High Falls. "As children, we crossed here many times. We'd hold hands and cross one way, then the other," McCotter says, "but we never went any further on foot."

McCotter doesn't remember meeting anyone other than the families at the lodge when she was here. Each family had their own time at the lodge and did not share the building with other groups. Her life revolved around swimming, hiking and socializing. When the owners sold the land to the DuPont Corporation, McCotter was about fifteen years old. All the teens in her group were sad. While this was not the end of their friendships, they certainly understood that it was the end of their visits to Buck Forest. Since the group came from Marion, North Carolina, they stayed in touch over the years and even visited the forest together.

WHO WAS ALEX GUION?

Alex Guion did not have as illustrious a pedigree as Frank Coxe. He did not inherit Guion Farm, the large flat area in the northern part of the forest; he bought it late in life. Yet his family name will live on in a prominent section of the forest. Guion Farms is a popular access area; there's also the Guion Trail and the Guion Farm Connector. No feature is named "Coxe" in the forest, although there's Coxe Avenue and Short Coxe in Asheville.

Guion had what only now we would call a privileged childhood. He grew up in Charlotte, North Carolina, in the late nineteenth century and went to boarding school in Massachusetts. After graduating in civil engineering from VPI in Blacksburg, Virginia—the Virginia Tech of today—he went into the construction business with his older brother. A 1915 society page from the *Charlotte News* described his wedding reception "elegant in every way" and the groom "a gentleman in fibre and in act." Alex and his bride, Anne, honeymooned in Western North Carolina. Maybe this is the first time Guion saw the beauty and potential of the mountain area.

Alex Guion and his older brother formed A.H. Guion & Company General Contractors. In 1914, they offered "the Beauty of Electricity." In the same year, Guion placed an ad regarding indoor toilets in the *Gastonia*

Gazette, the local newspaper from a small town outside Charlotte. The contractors stressed that the "health of the family demands that bath-rooms and water-closets, sinks, etc., be in perfect order, with no chance of sewer gas or foul air existing."

By the time Alex Guion bought what we know as Guion Farm in 1951, he was no longer installing bathrooms in private homes. His company had just become the lowest bidder to build the Margaret R. Pardee Memorial Hospital in Hendersonville. His company had bid $477,000. It took two years to finish the building and move patients into the new hospital's seventy-bed capacity.

The 5,411-acre farm that Guion bought has a colorful history—or, more precisely, colorful owners. Ownership can be traced back to George Holmes in the late nineteenth century. George Holmes was born in England, the son of a gentleman. After marrying Georgiana, they took off for Ontario, Canada. The family went back and forth back to Great Britain but finally immigrated to Henderson County. Their son, John, was fourteen years old when they arrived in the United States. John Holmes attended the new Yale School of Forestry. Eventually, he came back to North Carolina. By that time, the North Carolina Forest Service had just been set up to help fight fires. John Holmes became the first state forester, serving the state for thirty-seven years. Holmes Educational State Forest, a 235-acre strip of land, was named after him. The forest is located on Crab Creek Road, a little north of DuPont Forest.

By the early 1900s, all the lumber had been cut in the Midwest. Lumber barons looking for more opportunities came to the Southern Appalachians. Their effect was felt all over the area, including what later became Great Smoky Mountains National Park and Pisgah National Forest. Local owners sold their land to larger outside interests. Louis Carr bought almost seventy thousand acres from George Vanderbilt in 1912, becoming the largest employer in Transylvania County. The Gloucester Lumber Company was created when Joseph Silversteen purchased twenty thousand acres also from George Vanderbilt. George Holmes was part of this movement, albeit on a smaller scale, when he sold his land to Michigan lumbermen.

In a few decades, midwestern timber interests had moved on, presumably after they had cut all the trees they could. Harry Richard Playford, a colorful character from St. Petersburg, Florida, saw the Guion land as one more business opportunity. Playford, who had been a pilot in World War I, ran an aviation school. His best decision was to marry Elisabeth Coates, whose

Settlers and Land Barons

Sky Brook Ice Cream ad. *Courtesy of Friends of DuPont Forest.*

mother had been left a wealthy widow. Along with purchasing the Central National Bank in St. Petersburg, running an airline and other businesses, which were all funded by his mother-in-law, Playford purchased a summer home along the French Broad.

Playford bought land that would become the Guion Farm and created Sky Brook Farms. He bred a prize-winning line of Guernsey cows and advertised his ice cream, Guernsey Maid. The advertisement didn't need any adjective of praise. In 1951, Playford's Sky Brook Farm declared bankruptcy. His 5,411 acres was mostly pastureland. He sold the whole property to Alex Guion for "$10 and other considerations," which likely means that they did not want to disclose the price by writing it into the deed.

APPALACHIANS MAKE GOOD WORKERS

DuPont Corporation followed a long list of industries that moved to Western North Carolina. The good water, air and large expanse of low-cost land were certainly main draws. And so were the workers. In *The French Broad*, a book published in 1955, Wilma Dykeman writes about the French Broad River region in Western North Carolina and East Tennessee. She's best known for calling attention to the polluted river at the time, but she also discusses the industrial base of the area. Champion paper was established in 1906 to provide wood pulp for an Ohio paper mill. The company went through many transitions, but it is still here, employing a thousand workers in Canton; it's the largest employer in Haywood County.

Enka was established by a Dutch textile company in 1928 in Buncombe County, outside Asheville. It manufactured rayon. Again, water was the original attraction to the site, but willing, capable workers turned out to be a big asset. "Appalachian workers were a settled people," Dykeman writes. Most men owned their land and were not about to move for new prospects.

In 1902, Joseph Silversteen and his family came from Pennsylvania to what is now the town of Rosman in Transylvania County. He started a tanning operation and then the Gloucester Lumber Company by buying twenty thousand acres of forest land from George and Edith Vanderbilt. Silversteen paid his employees in scrip, money that could only be used in the company store in Rosman. Still, as Sara Lela Lutz points out in her master's dissertation, it was more buying power than most would have working anywhere else at the time.

"Rosman should have been the big town in the area," Earle Johnson, an early DuPont employee said. "But Silversteen built this large house which brought prestige to Brevard." The Silvermont Mansion, completed in 1917, was willed to the county in 1972 and has been a county park ever since.

The Ecusta paper mill was the inspiration and innovation of Harry Straus, a German immigrant. Like E.I. du Pont with explosives, Straus, almost 130 years later, saw that cigarette paper, a French product, could be improved and manufactured in the United States. Before Straus's work, cigarette paper was made in France from linen rags. Since linen is made from flax, why not go to the source of flax?

Ecusta means "rippling waters" in the Cherokee language. Again, water was a crucial component of linen production. A site on the Davidson River was chosen for cigarette paper production. At its height, Ecusta had almost two thousand employees. They made fine, thin papers like cigarette paper, Bible paper and, later, food-grade cellophane. Dykeman quotes a lawyer in Brevard, "Let some folks holler about industry and pollution of streams; for us it's dollars on Saturday."

In 1945, Harry Straus bought Camp Sapphire and created a recreation site for his employees. "The camp was fabulous," recalls a former employee. "It had a baseball team which played other plants, a baseball diamond, tennis courts, basketball. It was for employees but others in the area could use it." It also had a lake—what is a camp without a lake?

Ecusta's monthly employee newsletter, *The Echo*, shows pictures of children's Christmas parties in the 1940s. There were so many children that five separate parties were needed. Due to segregation during this time, a separate Christmas party was held for the children of African American employees. Although Harry Straus and his top management came from the North, Ecusta was set up along segregated lines. Straus believed that "if it's good for the community, it's good for Ecusta."

The company went through several name changes and buyouts—Olin, Olin Mathieson Chemical Corporation, Glatfelter—but is always referred to as Ecusta. In 1994, Glatfelter, the next-to-last owner, sold Camp Straus to developers. It became Straus Park, an upscale housing development. The

Settlers and Land Barons

Straus Lake was originally built for Ecusta employees. *Author's collection.*

last owner of the business, Purico Ltd., bought the Ecusta paper plant in 2001 and closed it a year later. The site is fenced off and still in need of environmental cleanup.

In 1956, President Dwight D. Eisenhower was headed for his second term in office. *Brown v. Board of Education of Topeka*, a landmark 1954 Supreme Court case, ruled unanimously that racial segregation of children in public schools was unconstitutional. But the composition of southern public schools had not yet changed. By the time DuPont Corporation came looking for property in North Carolina, the land had two major owners, Alex Guion and Frank Coxe. Both seemed happy to sell. Now the company had pure air, pure water and a pool of good, steady local workers at the Brevard site. It was ready to build a plant.

PART III
DuPont Corporation Goes to Work

IMMIGRANT IRÉNÉE STARTS AN EMPIRE

While the Coxe family had already bought land in the "Carolana," Pierre Samuel du Pont had become a nobleman because of his work with Louis XVI, the last king of France. By receiving the *noblesse de lettres* in 1784, he was able to add "de Nemours" to his name. Nemours, the du Ponts' ancestral home, is a small town located a ninety-minute drive south of Paris.

At the time, Antoine Lavoisier, a family friend, was the greatest scientist of the day. Now considered the father of modern chemistry, Lavoisier worked on the role oxygen plays in combustion. He recognized and named oxygen and hydrogen. He also improved gunpowder and became the superintendent of the French government's gunpowder plant.

Eleuthère Irénée, one of Pierre Samuel's sons, apprenticed under Lavoisier to learn how to manufacture gunpowder. It was a chaotic, lawless time in France. The well-to-do could not protect themselves from gang violence. Even with his accomplishments, Lavoisier did not survive the French Revolution. He was executed when the judge declared, "*La Republique n'a pas besoin de savants*" ("The Republic has no need for geniuses"). After their house was sacked by a mob, the extended du Pont family immigrated to the United States. They arrived in Newport, Rhode Island, on January 1, 1800.

When the family tried to decide what business to pursue, Irénée, as he was known, saw that American gunpowder was much poorer quality than in France. He found his niche in making and selling improved gunpowder. Irénée looked at various sites near Washington, D.C., for his gunpowder factory but found the ideal site on Brandywine Creek, in present-day Wilmington, Delaware. In 1802, the E.I. du Pont de Nemours company was formed. Two years later, it offered gunpowder for sale.

Early on, the mill had its first explosion. Safety became a major concern, a concern that is still emphasized today. At the time, workers walking into the plant had to turn out their pockets to show that they were not carrying matches. Still, a few years later, an explosion killed several workers, the first casualties. Irénée soon created a pension plan for widows and orphans.

The DuPont enterprise really took off during the War of 1812. It sold gunpowder to the fledging United States fighting against the British, who were intent on recapturing their lost colony. The cooperation between DuPont and its adopted country may have been the start of the military-industrial complex.

The British thought that Wilmington was a good starting point for an attack on Philadelphia. The British would target the gunpowder factories to disable their enemies. It became obvious that the United States military was not going to defend Wilmington. The du Ponts organized a militia to protect the city and its valuable manufacturing. Men who worked for the gunpowder plants and others from nearby textile mills planned to take on the British navy, but the invasion never happened.

After Irénée's death, his three sons took over the family business, creating a partnership. They improved the manufacturing process, making gunpowder kegs more moisture resistant. The company prospered with the Mexican-American War in 1846–48. There was always another conflict that could use gunpowder. During the Civil War, the DuPont partnership—not yet a corporation—sold black powder to the United States military.

Lammot du Pont, grandson of the founder of the business, went to the University of Pennsylvania to study chemistry and patented an improved gunpowder formula. When Alfred Nobel invented dynamite in 1867 and patented it in the United States a year later, Lammot convinced his business partners that they should make dynamite. DuPont bought the rights to manufacture dynamite, and Lammot started the Repauno plant in New Jersey for dynamite production. In 1894, Lammot was killed in a dynamite explosion.

At this point, DuPont, which had been a partnership, incorporated in Wilmington. Over the years, it became a multinational chemical company that diversified into many other products. It adopted the slogan "Better

DuPont Corporation Goes to Work

living through chemistry." DuPont used this phrase until 1982, when, by that time, the slogan was used ironically to mean mood-changing drugs, legal or otherwise.

The company bought new technology, improved on it and was able to commercialize the product. Rayon, nylon, spandex, Kevlar, Teflon, Corian countertops and other synthetics are now household names. But DuPont still kept its core explosive business, supplying the military for both world wars. DuPont Corporation was not without controversy—some DuPont products were cited for causing environmental and health problems.

In 1994, DuPont Corporation created the Land Legacy Program, whose purpose was to give away, sell at bargain prices or somehow preserve land that the company no longer needed. The program conserves green spaces for future generations. That same year, the company donated the one-thousand-acre Willow Grove Lake property to the Nature Conservancy of New Jersey. The conservancy created a preserve, which it still manages, offering trails and limited hunting. Since then, DuPont Corporation has donated land all over the world.

Mountain bikers at top speed. *Courtesy of Jim Parham.*

One of the largest donations occurred at the Okefenokee National Wildlife Refuge. In the 1990s, DuPont Corporation bought sixteen thousand acres adjacent to the refuge. The Okefenokee Swamp was created as a "refuge and breeding ground for migratory birds and other wildlife." The company planned to mine titanium dioxide, a mineral used in foods and pharmaceuticals. But people were concerned about its possible impact on the water supply. The company could not prove that there would not be an effect on the swamp. It changed its plans and eventually donated all the land to The Conservation Fund (TCF). Some of the acreage enlarged the Okefenokee Swamp, and the rest was put under a conservation easement with the Georgia National Wildlife Refuge.

In 2015, the company merged with Dow Chemicals, forming DowDuPont. Less than two years later, DowDuPont split three ways. Dow specializes in chemicals, chemical additives and packaging. DuPont focuses on specialty materials; its most recognizable product is Tyvek. Corteva Agriscience is an agricultural chemicals and seed company. Corteva is now responsible for cleaning up the Brevard plant. Through all the changes in names and owners, it is always referred to as the DuPont plant.

DUPONT CORPORATION COMES TO WESTERN NORTH CAROLINA

DuPont Corporation was attracted to the Brevard site for its pure water and air. At the time, these conditions were needed to manufacture hyper pure silicon for the nascent semiconductor industry. In 1956, the company bought 5,359 acres from Frank Coxe and smaller owners in Transylvania County and 5,411 acres from Alex Guion in Henderson County. The property also included some parcels that were not contiguous to the main purchase. The company hired local men to clear the land for construction.

DuPont Corporation brought down men from its other locations, chosen for their expertise. Leslie Grogan, the first plant manager, already had twenty-three years with the company and had handled an atomic energy project in World War II. The silicon plant needed engineers, but it also needed support staff since it was going to be self-contained. Paychecks were not going to come from headquarters in Delaware. By 1958, the Brevard plant had a payroll of $1.5 million annually. It prided itself on paying in the

DuPont Corporation Goes to Work

Original DuPont water tower for the silicon plant. *Courtesy of the Rowell Bosse North Carolina Room, Transylvania County Library.*

upper bracket of comparable jobs in the area. Its benefits package was also at the top of the scale.

And they were all men. Grogan was described as a twenty-three-year man—that meant that he had worked for DuPont for that long. Women would not be hired until much later for any position other than traditional office jobs. In the early days, the company was reluctant to send down single men to Western North Carolina. In the 1950s, southern women married young, mostly right after high school. If a single man relocated here, where was he going to find a suitable spouse?

Don Blankenship came as the first employee relations supervisor. At his retirement party, Blankenship remembers that his office was located on top of a garage in Brevard since they had not built the plant yet. Everyone was eager to get a job with DuPont. The company was already well known for its high safety standards. Eager young men still in their teens were looking for their first job. Supplies were bought locally, which boosted the local economy. With $2.5 million of annual purchases, the company needed a professional purchasing agent.

Like many northern companies coming to the South, DuPont Corporation wanted to avoid having to deal with industrial unions. Good wages and benefits were important, but it took other precautions. Two entrances to the plant site were built. One was for the employees, and the other was for construction workers. If construction workers were unionized and had a strike, they could only block their own entrance and not the DuPont employee entrance.

While constructing the plant, the company also removed Buck Forest Lodge, which Ellen McCotter, Amelia Bond and their friends so loved. A worker who was interviewed many years after his retirement expressed

Aerial view of DuPont plant, 1979. *Courtesy of the North Carolina Forest Service.*

surprise that the lodge had not been refurbished for executives and guests. The view from the lodge was spectacular. But he may not have realized how run-down and erratic the building was. Haphazard and unpredictable running water and electricity might have seemed charming and nostalgic to Buck Forest children, but by the later 1950s, it would not have been amusing to executives and their families from urban areas.

DuPont Corporation also did not want anything on its property that would attract outsiders; it established clear property boundaries. Before DuPont bought the property, the land had been private as well—as private before as it was now. Still, the boundaries then may not have been clearly marked or patrolled, and poachers probably hunted or fished on the land. Now the company clearly posted its property.

In the early 1960s, the DuPont plant and other manufacturing in Transylvania County put wage earners above the national average. In 1964, national weekly earnings were $102.97, while the Transylvania average was $108.99. Transylvania County was a good place to work.

The Brevard plant published an employee relations supervisory newsletter. At first, it was a weekly mimeographed newsletter that went out to all supervisors to be shared with their staff. It was a mixture of company policies, plant news and cute jokes of the day. The company recognized that many employees were new to the area and needed some information on how to sign up to vote and where to register the family car. It had reminders like:

> *Another reminder—when an employee has been off sick, he should check through medical before returning to work.*
>
> *On Saturday May 1, we will have X-ray technicians (women) visit our plant for a tour.…These folks are from a Johnson City hospital and they use 100% of DuPont X-ray film.*

The newsletter was always lightened up with witticisms:

> *No wonder today's teenagers get mixed up. Half the adults are telling him to find himself and the other half to get lost.*

The jokes at women's expense were not funny at the time and would be considered unacceptable not too far in the future. Service anniversaries were very important. In 1965, the newsletter pointed out that fourteen years was the average service at DuPont—obviously not all in Brevard. It concluded that "Stability is a condition at DuPont."

Although informative, the two-page mimeographed sheets did not have the capability to publish photographs. The problem was solved when they switched to a multi-page color newsletter, which they titled *Fotofax*. One of the first issues celebrated ten years since the opening of the Brevard plant.

Much of the news involved announcements and endearments from the DuPont Employees Recreation Association (DERA). The organization was started in 1963, with management approval. For two dollars in the mid-1960s, a DERA membership got a family a "Kiddie Xmas party, Easter Egg hunt, DERA dance, Fishing in Little River, Hiking, Barn for horses, Picnic....And the list goes on."

At a picnic for the Dupont plant Technical Department, September 1981. *Courtesy of Bob Delwiche.*

DERA promised summer fun opportunities with streams, waterfalls and trails to fish, hunt, picnic, hike or sightsee. Before the trout fishing season opened in the spring, employees were reminded that they had to be a member of DERA to participate. They paid one dollar for ten trout. DuPont stocked the Little River, so fishermen had a good chance to get ten. But before going hiking or fishing, they needed to check at the gatehouse. "Patrolmen have snake bite kits on loan." Former employees remember DERA as a genuine country club for themselves, their families and guests.

But a country club needs someplace to swim. Employees and their families all knew about Straus Lake, owned by the Ecusta plant located a few miles north; many had been there as guests. In 1973, *Fotofax* announced that a new lake for employees would be built. The chair of the lake committee made it clear that this ambitious plan would depend on other priorities and work parties willing to help. The lake was opened two years later with a four-hundred-foot dock and fourteen campsites. Activities included boating, picnicking, fishing, tennis courts and, of course, swimming.

CHANNING HUBBARD, THE FIRST SITE EMPLOYEE

"I'm the only living person who knows DuPont in Brevard from beginning to end," Chan Hubbard says. He grew up in Western North Carolina and started working for the DuPont site in 1956. When he returned from a stint in the army at twenty-one, he was hired as one of three men to clear the future plant site. "They hired me because I had learned about explosives in the military," Hubbard says.

He first worked on building roads and then moved to construction. He cut down trees and laid out the parking lot. To work at DuPont Corporation, a person needed a high school education. When asked about segregation at the plant, he recalls that "the schools were segregated but DuPont was integrated." Other employees give a much different account of DuPont's beginnings in Brevard.

Hubbard had many assignments in his thirty-seven years with the company, but he cites checking property boundaries as the most challenging part of his career. Property lines may have been a little looser and less well defined before DuPont Corporation moved in. Hubbard had to survey the forty-one miles that defined the DuPont lands at the time. The motto was "Trim it, Paint it, Post it."

As he inspected the boundaries, he found buildings, fence lines and pastures encroaching on the DuPont property. If an adjoining landowner had inadvertently built on company land, Hubbard made him sign a document so that he realized he had pushed outside his property, but he was not forced to remove the structure. "In some cases," Hubbard says, "we changed the property lines to accommodate the neighbors. Other times, we kept the boundaries as they had been."

Ecusta, the other major plant in the area, had unionized in 1971. It was only a matter of time until DuPont hourly employees attempted to organize at the Brevard Plant. Channing was charged with talking to the men to learn what their problems were. Hubbard became a counselor for Human Resources. "Employees gained confidence in me that I would not go back and tell management what they said," Hubbard says.

"At the time in the 1970s," Hubbard recalls, "mechanics were making twelve dollars an hour. That was good money then, more than all the other companies in the area." DuPont management thought that since Chan Hubbard was local, he would understand the local people. Hubbard was a one-man Union Avoidance officer. "I asked the men, 'What do you want a union for?'"

Chan Hubbard in the forest. *Courtesy of Chan Hubbard family.*

Hubbard recalls that management said to him, "We need to know how many people are going to vote for the union." He estimated "about fifty out of nine hundred." When the vote came in, only about forty-two voted for the union. During DuPont Corporation's time in Brevard, two union votes were taken, and both were against the union.

Hubbard's father-in-law had worked for the Ecusta plant. "Harry Straus was good to his people. He built a lake so that children of employees could swim," Hubbard says. "In the past, unions were needed to outlaw child labor and such. But not now." He feels that the demise of Ecusta was because of its union.

Hubbard helped establish the DuPont Employees Recreation Association. He wanted to encourage the employees and their families out into the forest to hike, see the waterfalls and picnic. "Employees could take visitors on the property to hike, fish, camp," Hubbard says. "They had it made." To enjoy these activities, they had to sign in with security at the plant gatehouse "so that they knew where the employees were." There were two people working at the gatehouse 24/7. One stayed at the gatehouse, and the other patrolled the property. Hubbard's favorite personal pastimes were fishing and riding a four-wheeler.

Hubbard helped build a baseball field across Staton Road, the remains of which can still be seen from Sheep Mountain Trail opposite the entrance to the High Falls Access Area. He was so involved with this project that the field was named after him, Hubbard Field. Chan Hubbard cut the ribbon on opening day in 1974.

In 1991, Hubbard was laid up in the hospital in Augusta, Georgia, for several months. "When Chan was ill, he asked for pictures of the waterfalls. It let him escape," says his daughter, Connie Hubbard Corn. At the annual company picnic in August 1991, the employees made a video for Hubbard while he was in the hospital. The thirteen-minute video, shot with a jerky hand-held camera, is still on YouTube. Most employees are wearing dark-blue T-shirts that say "Pride in People."

The video shows a band playing in the gazebo and men in dunking booths. Lots of food, balloons and soda. A young woman times two men who are cutting a thick log with a two-man crosscut saw. A big sign on the side of a van reads "Get Well Soon Chan. We Miss You." The bulk of the video consists of employees and their spouses wishing Hubbard a quick recovery. One man encapsulates all the messages when he faces the camera and says, "Chan, we need you back at the plant. The place can't go on without you." Hubbard came back to work but retired in 1992 after more than thirty-six years of service. Now at eighty-three, he's enjoying his great-grandchildren.

MAKING HYPERPURE SILICON

We think of silicon (Si) as sand. There's plenty of it on the earth, although it does not exist by itself. In nature, the element is in chemical combination with oxygen and other elements and known as silicon dioxide or quartz. A DuPont memo, "Hyper Pure Silicon," dated July 1957, explains that silicon composes 28 percent of Earth's crust, second only to oxygen in abundance. Silicon is used to regulate the flow of electrical current.

During World War II, DuPont Corporation produced high-purity silicon for the electronics industry, including diodes in radar equipment. It located the first plant in Newport, Delaware, and made silicon under government sponsorship. After the war, the company was no longer interested in this business. In 1952, the company received an order from Bell Telephone Laboratories for three hundred pounds of silicon. If the general public knows anything about Bell Labs, it's that it invented the transistor in 1948; it was the research arm of AT&T. Bell Laboratories is now owned by Nokia, a Finnish company.

The potential for transistors was unlimited. A transistor is more rugged than its predecessor, the vacuum tube, more reliable and can withstand shock. Silicon chips would replace bulky and unreliable vacuum tubes in consumer products such as industrial machinery, radios and the nascent television. Just as important to Bell Labs, it would improve telephone service.

Now silicon was needed on a commercial scale. The company had continued to make silicon at Newport in a semiworks plant, sized halfway between a laboratory and a full commercial plant. When pure, the element is not a good insulator or conductor. But the process starts with pure silicon. Then some impurities are added, as counterintuitive as this may sound. Semiconductor-grade silicon cost $380 per pound in 1957, which is more than $3,538 today. But only a tiny sliver is needed for a transistor.

In late 1957, DuPont Corporation put out a memo on "Silicon and Its Uses." It was a "gee whizz" look at the potential of silicon:

> *The electrical world now sees hyper pure silicon as a powerful new electronic tool. Electronics, a scientific wonder of our time, has a future more dazzling than its past with applications of an unlimited potential staggering our imagination.*

The company became the first commercial manufacturer of semiconductor-grade silicon, a large new industry. Since the Newport plant was not adequate,

DuPont Corporation Goes to Work

DuPont Corporation built a plant in Brevard to produce high-grade silicon. The company was attracted to the Brevard site because of its pure water and air. At the time, there was very little industry other than logging in the area. The Brevard Tannin Company was located in Pisgah Forest, closely allied with logging.

DuPont Corporation was looking for a pure site. It wanted undeveloped land with no neighboring industry. The 10,500-acre tract between Hendersonville and Brevard seemed ideal. But where to locate the plant itself within that large expanse of property? The logical place would have been the Guion Farm in Henderson County, which is flat and with reasonable road access. Instead, the DuPont plant was built in the Transylvania County section of its newly acquired property. Specifically, it located the buildings in the horseshoe part of Little River.

Operator at DuPont's new silicon plant at Brevard, North Carolina, "picking" silicon needles. This method of inspection helps maintain the high purity standards of DuPont silicon. The material, a non-metallic element, is used in such devices as transistors, diodes and rectifiers, which in turn are used in manufacturing more compact, more efficient communication and electronic equipment. While silicon and its compound are well known in the industry, it is the pure element developed by DuPont research that has become important in the electronics field. *Courtesy of the Hagley Museum and Library.*

Some say that the reason was that Henderson County taxes were higher than in Transylvania County. Others mention that Henderson County had better employment opportunities, including a new GE plant, and Transylvania County residents could use the work.

The company pointed out that since it was not in the electronic business, the development of uses for silicon depended on its evaluation by customers' experience in this field. DuPont continued research on the production process. According to Bob Delwiche, who spent his whole career at DuPont Corporation, up until the middle of 1958 DuPont Corporation was the sole supplier of high-grade silicon. But not for long. The competition was catching up and surpassing it.

WHAT TO DO WITH ALL THIS LAND?

By 1962, silicon was no longer a competitive product for DuPont's Brevard plant. DuPont Corporation shut down the silicon operation and started building facilities to manufacture X-ray film. AB Morrison, a manager from Parlin, New Jersey, came down to Western North Carolina to head the new Photo Products Division.

Almost as soon as Morrison became the new plant manager, he wrote an eleven-page memo wondering what the company should do with its eleven thousand acres. In a few months, the new Photo Products Division would inherit a huge amount of mountain property. The land may have been necessary years ago to keep air and water free from contamination during DuPont's silicon-production days, but now it seemed like just a managerial burden. Morrison writes:

> *A question remains—"What can and should be done with the thousands of acres of property in excess of present and forecast specific Photo Products photographic film manufacturing needs?" This pertinent question soon (after arrival) strikes each new technical supervisory transferee (from our more confined plant in the Northeast).*

Morrison took this question seriously. He spent many hours traversing and inspecting the property. Coming from Central New Jersey, he may not have been familiar with a wilderness of this size. The terrain was described as "rolling with gentle slopes but with some abrupt, steep rocky ridges with elevation from 2,200 feet to 3,800 feet." The most outstanding feature is the water—small rivulets and streams feed into the Little River. But it was the waterfalls that made this property stand out.

Previous owners had built some trails. Timber companies also added to the network of roads and paths. DuPont needed roads for fire protection. Morrison looked for advice on the feasibility of making a profit from timber, but he was not reassured. The North Carolina Forestry Department is quoted as saying: "The forest condition of much of the area is such that natural reproduction of desirable species is extremely unlikely. Nonetheless, a combined saw timber-pulpwood operation is feasible."

Morrison realized that the area attracted both tourists and retirees—not as much as Asheville, maybe, but Brevard could not be far behind. It implied that DuPont land might be a gold mine. "For DuPont not to realize a satisfactory return (on sale of land in the future—if this is the final recourse) is difficult to contemplate."

There was a lot of land here. Morrison saw the potential for several industrial plants. The memo recaps the history. The acreage listed in the document may not be exact, but the gross numbers were good enough for Morrison's purposes. By 1956, the company had purchased two main properties:

- Guion Farm, fed by Grassy Creek
- Buck Forest, containing the Little River Basin; several owners were involved, but Frank Coxe was the primary seller

The company was able to buy both tracts of land for $20 per acre, for a total cost of $225,000. First, the plant was going to be on the Guion Farm site. The North Carolina Highway Commission agreed to pave Sky Valley road. When the company moved the site location to the present Buck Forest site in Brevard, the highway commission paved US 276.

To Morrison, land boundaries were fixed and unalterable. To the neighbors around the DuPont land, boundaries were a little more fluid. People living locally may have been accustomed to hunting and fishing on private land. But now there were hard property lines and the staff to enforce it. Controlling trespassers and poachers seemed to be a constant headache. Even Morrison admitted that not all of the perimeter was surveyed in 1956 when the property was purchased, something that would be unheard of today.

When DuPont Corporation came in, it planted 500,000 white pine seedlings, which cost $10,375. Earle Johnson, who came to the Brevard

Road slide on US 276 after the 1964 storm. *Courtesy of the Rowell Bosse North Carolina Room, Transylvania County Library.*

site in 1957, remembers seeing local women bent over planting small trees on the Guion property. The property, a former farm, was flat and cleared. "Men didn't want to do this kind of work," Johnson said.

There was also the cost of fire protection and maintaining roads and trails. To Morrison, an engineer, dealing with this land may have been bewildering. He outlined three options:

- The land could just be left alone. But that costs money with fire control, maintaining roads and trails and dealing with trespassers and poachers. People shut out of the property would resent that the land was just standing here and not used.
- Why not just sell the land? But DuPont Corporation would get neighbors, and streams might get contaminated. This idea was quickly rejected.
- Why not put the land to use and start a timber operation? It was not in the mainstream of DuPont's business, but all the other conditions appeared to be in place.

It seemed that the more accessible timber had been heavily cut before DuPont Corporation acquired the land. In addition, it takes twenty to forty years for white pine to go from seed to cut timber. But Morrison decided to keep the land and attempt to bring in some income from selling the wood.

Morrison did not want to lay out any company money on this venture. The first section considered was a two-hundred-acre area recently hit by lightning, which started a fire. A local logger surveyed the land and agreed to plant white pine seedlings, at a cost of $1,200. Since the wood now on the acreage would return $1,900, the effort would realize a small, immediate profit.

With such a large amount of land, there was bound to be fires. Morrison's memo only talks about fire control and suppression—nothing about controlled burns, a philosophy not yet widespread in 1962. If there was a fire on DuPont's property, the North Carolina Forest Service would take over responsibility and then bill the property owner. That happened in the spring of 1962, a few months before this memo was written. Morrison felt a need to state that the bill was paid.

When the previous silicon management passed the company baton to Photo Products, it also passed on the "No Trespassing" rule. This created a lot of resentment from the local population who wanted to hunt, hike and fish on this vast property. It also encouraged illegal poachers, whom DuPont did not think were worth prosecuting.

If DuPont Corporation created controlled access, responsible hunters would take out some of the game, making it less attractive to poachers. It was difficult to come up with a policy that allowed visitors access to the land. The DuPont Company consulted with the Poinsett Lumber Company, which maintained an open-land policy. The lumber company did not seem to have a problem with allowing visitors on its land. Morrison was uncomfortable with that but left the window cracked open for further review. The bottom-line decisions were to put the land to work and keep the "No Trespassing" rule.

To add to Morrison's problems, Frank Coxe, a former landowner, reappeared. Coxe wanted access to some of the DuPont land he had sold for personal hunting and fishing trips. He claimed that the company representative during the land transfer told him "it would be no problem," a statement that was categorically denied. Coxe wanted to buy back two thousand acres of the best land in the Little River basin. Coxe felt he was "done in" by the purchase and was spreading his views in both Asheville, where he lived, and in Brevard. Morrison ended his memo with, "We may further expect to hear adverse criticism."

When DuPont Corporation bought the property, it hired Charlie Paxton, a professional forest ranger. Paxton was a descendant of one of the original families who settled in Transylvania County more than two hundred years ago. He grew up in Rosman, a small town south of Brevard. Before coming to manage the thousands of company acres, Paxton had years of experience with the North Carolina Forest Service.

The land was abused by haphazard logging, farming and fires. It was the same condition that Carl Schenk found when he surveyed George Vanderbilt's land more than sixty years earlier. Since there were only five miles of roads on the original property, fire and logging roads were needed quickly. In a 1977 interview, Paxton stated that there was now a network of forty miles of trails and roads.

Paxton upgraded the forest by switching from hardwoods to evergreens, mostly white pine. As related in Morrison's memo, this was paid for by logging and selling the wood already on the property. DuPont management made it clear that the forest had to pay for itself. Paxton planted acres of white pine on abandoned pastureland on the Guion Farm. The company also hired Champion Paper to harvest timber from other parts of the property.

Looking for fish at Lake Dense. *Author's collection.*

Paxton supervised the building of Lake Dense in about 1978. There had been a small lake there, dug by the Coxe family, one of the previous property owners. Although the lake had some water, small trees were growing in the lakebed. Employees cleared the lake of trees. An outside company replaced part of the dam. Lake Julia provided some water via a pipe to help maintain water level in Lake Dense.

At a staff get-together in the mid-1970s, Charlie Paxton declared Jack Dense, the plant manager, a true citizen of the South. Dense, who came from New Jersey, mentioned that he had never eaten 'possum and therefore was not a true southerner. Paxton obliged by getting a live 'possum from another employee and fattened it up. He then cooked the 'possum "southern style." He anointed all the attendees at the get-together at the Guion Farmhouse "true citizens of the South." In the account published in *Fotofax*, DuPont's local house organ, no recipes were offered.

It seems that the large tract of land that DuPont Corporation was sitting on was still a dilemma in the 1980s. A memo from an employee relation supervisor in 1984 relates that he was disappointed that the company was not going to participate in the Natural Heritage program. Today, the program inventories properties to learn the ecological significance of the sites. It may identify rare plants and animals.

Then the memo veers to discussing a proposal to donate the entire property to the state for tax purposes. The employee relations supervisor opposed that move because both employees and customers used the land for recreation. This benefit was considered a competitive advantage for marketing X-ray film.

Still, in 1986, five parcels of DuPont land were appraised for their possible easement or sales value. A conservation easement is defined as a voluntary, legal agreement that permanently limits uses of the land in order to protect its conservation values. It protects the land from development in perpetuity. The owner gets a tax benefit while still owning the property.

A Hooker Falls and Sheep Mountain tract of 848 acres was considered the most attractive for development and had the highest value per acre—$4,363. In contrast, the 1,365-acre piece that included Stone Mountain and Rocky Ridge had steep terrain with difficult access. About one-third of that land was planted in white pine that still had fifteen years to mature. It was evaluated at $1,201 per acre. The more interesting number might be the total value of all five tracts—$8.1 million—for less than 4,000 acres. That was much more than the amount that DuPont Corporation received for almost twice that acreage ten years later.

MOVING ON TO X-RAY FILM

The DuPont Company has been involved with producing film since the 1910s. It introduced its X-ray film in 1932. Cronar film was first developed in Parlin, New Jersey, but DuPont needed a larger facility. It designed the Brevard plant to produce Cronar polyester base and Cronex medical X-ray films. Much of the market for medical film was for mammograms and chest X-rays. According to the American Cancer Society, modern mammography methods were developed late in the 1960s and first officially recommended in 1976. The demand for X-ray film was high. DuPont created a colorful booklet for the general public to explain what went on in its Brevard plant. It describes the film process in three parts.

1. The first step creates Cronar, the film base. Dimethyl terephthalate (DMT) and ethylene glycol is reacted to make the polymer for Cronar. The hot polymer is forced through a narrow slit onto a large turning wheel, cooled and then stretched to the right width, length and thickness. This becomes the base for X-ray film. DuPont also shipped Cronar to its Parlin site so it could be processed for the graphic arts industry. The Polaroid Corporation bought the film base to make instant photographic film.

The chemical name for the polyester film base is polyethylene terephthalate, often abbreviated as PET. The name for this polyester is the same whatever form the polymer is molded into, such as DuPont film (Cronar or Mylar), DuPont fibers like Dacron, soft drink bottles or many other forms. The melting point of PET is 265 degrees Centigrade, a very high temperature—consider that the boiling point of water is 100C.

This step of the process is done in regular light. The Cronar base production line was run continuously, except for major upgrades. The polymer had to be kept warm at all times to prevent it from permanently solidifying and gumming up the equipment.

2. The rest of the process is done in the dark—actually, in photographic safelight. The film base is coated with two gelatin coatings, one being the light-sensitive silver halide emulsion and the other a protective top coating. That's the working part of the film, and it is quite pressure sensitive. An anti-abrasion protective coating is added to both sides of the film to protect the emulsion layer. Engineers working on improving the process had to do their investigations in darkroom lighting. Working in the dark was a challenge to everyone involved in making and checking the product. The output is a roll of coated film that can weigh up to two tons. Wrapped rolls are moved by conveyors to either a storage or to a finishing area.

Equestrian on Covered Bridge. *Author's collection.*

"Sure. I'm in no hurry," he says and stops. I explain my search for the quarry. Dave the cyclist and I hunt for the quarry, but cyclists and hikers go at different speed. "I'll see if I can find it. I'll leave you a sign," Dave says, and he takes off. Soon he comes back around. "It's on an unmarked offshoot trail of Rocky Quarry Trail," Dave says.

The quarry isn't a big hole in the ground, as one would expect. Instead, carved-out cliffs protrude out in a random fashion, creating a modern

Rock quarry in DuPont Forest. *Author's collection.*

sculpture. Refrigerator-sized boulders also hide behind trees; it's been a while since this quarry has been used. This is where the rock came from when DuPont Road and Staton Road were built in the early 1970s. I've read that some climb the walls of the quarry without ropes or gear. There are handholds, if you're practiced at this kind of climbing. I can see where the rocks are very accessible from the trail, but I'll keep my feet on the ground.

BREVARD, PAST AND PRESENT, WITH STUART ENGLISH

When DuPont Corporation arrived in Brevard in 1956 to build its silicon plant, public accommodations in North Carolina was still segregated. The company owned other facilities in the South and had a policy of following community norms. In Brevard, it also took the lead from Ecusta, another local plant started by a northerner, which had been operating since 1939.

DuPont Corporation Goes to Work

In 1958, a two-page spread in the company-wide *Better Living* magazine showed how newly arrived DuPont employees and their families fit into the community: "DuPont wants to conform to community social and cultural patterns. It seeks to help in the development of communities where its plants are located." This is the environment that Earle Johnson found when he transferred from Illinois to the Brevard plant.

By the time Stuart English entered the ninth grade in 1963, the school had just become integrated. Stuart English's Transylvania County family history goes back for generations. One of his ancestors founded the English Chapel, now surrounded by Pisgah National Forest. His father was superintendent of Bent Creek Experimental Forest in Pisgah Forest just south of Asheville, and they lived in a forest service house. Once Stuart's father retired in 1963, he built a house on fifteen acres of land outside of Brevard that he inherited from his family. At the time, the Junior High School was located downtown where the Transylvania County Library is now.

Brevard's downtown businesses were focused on the everyday needs of its residents. A drive-in soda shop was located across from the old Junior High School. English remembers the fights that would develop outside. "Everyone

Historic Rosenwald area of Brevard. *Author's collection.*

had a car or knew someone who did," English says. In high school, he went to Straus Lake, the recreational park built for Ecusta employees and their guests, where he swam, hiked and hung around with friends.

Downtown Brevard also had several pharmacies, including Varner's Drugstore, which opened in 1942. It was a full-fledged drugstore with a soda counter. When Varner's closed in 1994, Dee Dee Parker turned the space into a gift shop. Later, the business expanded into Rocky's Grill and Soda shop. The counter is still here, and historic pictures of Varner's Drugstore line the wall.

Before integration, Transylvania County had several elementary schools for African American children but no high schools. Students were bused for forty-five minutes to Ninth Avenue High School in Hendersonville. These children had to travel out of the county even though their parents paid county taxes.

Today, in Brevard's Rosenwald Historic District, an African American elementary school was saved. The former school became the headquarters for the Transylvania County Board of Education. Former classrooms have been turned into offices where educators and officials now work. On the walls, pictures of the old segregated schools show children and one or two teachers proudly standing in front of their school on picture day.

A set of information boards line the main corridor and explain the history of segregated schools in Transylvania County. Starting in 1862, 447 enslaved individuals and 3 freedmen lived in the county. Could some have been residents of the Kingdom of the Happy Land? Jumping to 1960, the Transylvania Citizen Improvement Organization (TCIO) was formed to promote the educational, political and economic opportunities for African Americans in the county.

Two years later, the group approached the county school board for the right to have African American children go to public schools. The board offered token integration, but the group refused. They took their case to federal court in Asheville, where the judge ordered the Transylvania County Junior and High School desegregated by 1963. The elementary schools were not included in this ruling and did not integrate until they were forced to comply with the Civil Rights Act of 1964. Transylvania County was the first school system to integrate in the state and one of the first in the South.

DuPont Corporation Goes to Work

THE DUPONT PLANT WAS A GOOD PLACE TO WORK

"DuPont was a make-believe world," Skip (Arnold) Sheldon recalls. "Everyone worked hard." But all employees and their families also had the opportunity to play on the premises: swimming in Lake DERA, annual picnics that some describe as rivaling a county fair, hiking, fishing and camping on the premises—even a baseball field. Groups not connected to the DuPont plant could request to use the property as well.

DuPont Corporation supported the United Way in the area. It was also instrumental in building up Blue Ridge Community College. The college was used to educate the workforce with classes in both counties. DuPont chemists were often on the faculty. The Hendersonville YMCA building had lots of impetus from DuPont folks. There seemed to be no end to the company's largesse.

The Brevard DuPont plant was a good place to work. But as the saying goes, "All good things must come to an end."

Coater and emulsion area at the Brevard plant, 1962. *Courtesy of the Rowell Bosse North Carolina Room, Transylvania County Library.*

PART IV
Summit Camps

SUMMER CAMP, THE BEST PART OF CHILDHOOD

Summer camps have been a fixture of Western North Carolina for more than one hundred years. The area may be the most concentrated summer camp destination in the world. Camp Merrie-Woode in Sapphire has been teaching girls outdoor skills since 1919. Like most overnight camps, it offers swimming, crafts, archery, horseback riding and many other activities that are difficult for children to find back home. Currently, the tuition is $6,800 for its main July session, which lasts more than a month.

Often private camps are intergenerational enterprises. In Transylvania County, Eagle's Nest Camp was started by Alex Waite, head of psychology at Rollins College in Florida in 1945. Helen Waite, the next generation, served as director of Eagle's Nest. Her daughter, Noni, grew up at the camp and is now the camp's executive director.

The Summit Camps were a latecomer in the camping world. In 1967, Ben Cart bought 1,437 acres of land in Henderson and Transylvania Counties, including 40 acres from DuPont Corporation. On this land, he built two traditional summer camps, one for girls and one for boys. They were situated about a mile apart as the crow flies—close enough for approved co-ed activities.

Ben Cart grew up in Spartanburg. His father had helped develop Lake Summit, south of Hendersonville, as a summer getaway by impounding the Green River. Young Cart spent most of his summers swimming and water skiing on Lake Summit. In the mid-1950s, Cart founded Cart Petroleum and Cart Oil, which he started with a single fuel tanker. The business expanded to serve the Southeast. He then sold both companies to Hess Oil. Summit Camps were his next enterprise.
    Although the Summit Camps abutted the DuPont Corporation property, the camps had their own separate entrance from the plant. The access from Reasonover Road is currently a short distance northeast from the Fawn Lake Access Area. Parents brought their children through here and drove on Conservation Road. Today, this access is available to DuPont Forest visitors where an ornamental stone pillar still stands that heralded the camp entrance. Visitors don't usually approach the forest from this entrance since there is only space for one or two cars outside the forest. It's also a bit of a walk from here to most of the DuPont Forest attractions. Currently, concessionaires who offer activities on Lake Julia enter from here. Stand-up paddle boarding lessons are given on Lake Julia. The company brings its clients in vans along with its boards and drives on Conservation Road to the lake.
    When Cart bought the land, Lake Julia did not exist. But a summer camp needs a lake. In 1968, Ben Cart applied for a permit to build a dam on Reasonover Creek for a lake that would be the center of activities for both camps. The inflow of water from Briery Fork Creek and Reasonover Creek created a ninety-nine-acre lake that was named Lake Julia in honor of Ben Cart's first wife.
    Jones Garren, known as Dick, was Cart's right-hand man. Since Garren understood the topography of the land, he was instrumental in creating the camp's physical features. "He knew how water ran downhill," a current resident remembers. He hired a crew of local men and high school boys to clear the area of trees. The first few years the camp took shape, boys were expected to do some building in the morning. In the afternoon, they took part in traditional camp activities. During this time, they slept in large army-style tents.
    It was a small camp. An application form for the 1977 summer season stated that four weeks cost $570, the equivalent of $2,404 in 2019. Compared to today's private camps in Western North Carolina, Summit Camps would have been a bargain. The application also requested a photograph of the camper. Like summer camps today, campers could not receive food parcels or phone calls.

The girls' dining hall at Summit Camps is no longer standing. *Author's collection.*

Girls Camp was at the end of Lake Julia Road facing the lake. The centerpiece was the dining room, an octagonal wooden building with a surrounding covered porch. Six cabins slept seven girls and a camp counselor. Later, a cabin was built for CITs (Counselors in Training). The Boys Camp, up on a hill, had the same number of cabins.

Several buildings from the Girls Camp still survive. The girls' lodge is where girls gathered for rainy-day activities and snacking, as there was a small kitchen. At the beginning of the camp's life, Julia Cart cooked meals here. Later, food was driven down from the Boys Camp to the Girls Camp on large heated trays. The girls' lodge is now used by the forest service. Cart also built a boathouse, still standing, around the bend from the Girls Camp.

The Summit Camps infirmary was located above Lake Julia. After the Summit Camps closed permanently, DuPont Corporation decided to buy the land in order to gain access to another clean water source and to protect its boundaries from potentially undesirable neighbors. The infirmary was repurposed into guest rooms for DuPont Corporation

Stairs from Lake Julia to the DuPont Forest office. *Author's collection.*

visitors. The inn with seven bedrooms was quite comfortable. It's now the DuPont Forest office.

A 1977 multi-page brochure with separate inserts for each camp shows the different emphasis between the genders. The girls' section stressed that the girls' cozy cabins had indoor plumbing. Girls would be able to try horseback riding, canoeing, sailing and tennis. The Boys Camp brochure insert emphasizes plenty of challenges, as a boy is shown rappelling down into Lake Julia. In another photograph, a boy walks a tightrope over Lake Julia, holding on two ropes. If he fell, he would land in the water. Still, the photograph looks unnerving.

The Boys Camp was in a section of the DuPont Forest that is now off limits to visitors; no trails lead to this area. The boys' dining hall was made of wormy chestnut. Cart had a sawmill on his property, where much of the wood used by the camp was cut. The desk at the Aleen Steinberg Visitor Center is made with wood from the dining hall. Besides the boys' cabins and dining hall, Ben Cart built his private house here. He mounted a satellite dish on the Boys Camp's water tower to service his home. Another house

Above: Bridal Veil Falls. *Author's collection.*

Left: Young mountain bikers on the trail. *Courtesy of David Vance.*

Hooker Falls. *Author's collection.*

Cascade Lake, built for the Cascade Power Company. *Author's collection.*

Left: Triple Falls. *Author's collection*.

Below: View from Stone Mountain in the northeast corner of DuPont Forest. *Author's collection*.

Lake Alford. *Author's collection.*

The Silvermont Mansion in Brevard was completed in 1917. *Author's collection.*

Above: Jeff Jennings on Cedar Rock Mountain. *Courtesy of Jeff Jennings.*

Left: Wintergreen Falls. *Author's collection.*

Above: Hearts-a-Bustin' (strawberry bush) burst out in the fall. *Author's collection.*

Left: Tree in the donut hole. *Author's collection.*

Above: Lake DERA (DuPont Employees Recreation Association). *Author's collection.*

Right: Hiking in snow. *Author's collection.*

Mother and daughter mushrooms. *Author's collection.*

High Falls. *Author's collection.*

Above: Lake Julia was built for the Summit Camps. *Author's collection.*

Right: Buck Forest Lodge chimney, with Ellen McCotter, who stayed at the lodge as a child. *Author's collection.*

Above: Lake Dense. *Author's collection.*

Left: Forest Ranger Wes Sketo guides a tree walk. *Author's collection.*

Lake Julia boathouse. *Author's collection.*

Pink lady slipper. *Courtesy of Linda Spangler.*

Fawn Lake was built by Ben Cart for the Buck Forest Housing Development, which was never built. *Author's collection.*

DuPont Corporation Plant in Brevard. *Courtesy of the Rowell Bosse North Carolina Room, Transylvania County Library.*

Above: Biking on Conservation Road. *Author's collection.*

Left: Grassy Creek Falls. *Author's collection.*

Above: Lake Julia Spillway. *Author's collection.*

Left: Lower section of Triple Falls in ice. *Author's collection.*

At the top of Big Rock Trail. *Author's collection.*

View from the top of Cedar Rock Mountain. *Author's collection.*

Above: Lake Imaging. *Author's collection.*

Left: Natural corkscrew tree on a trail. *Author's collection.*

Summit Camps water tower. *Author's collection.*

utilized by his senior staff is now devoted to the forest supervisor and his family. Ben Cart's house was later torn down.

Boys and girls shared activity spaces such as the horse barn, riflery range and darkroom, but not at the same time. But there were some co-ed social times. Many activities occurred in the girls' dining hall beyond meals. On

Friday evenings, the boys would hike over to the Girls Camp for movie night. On Saturday evenings, the boys would come over to square dance in the girls' dining hall. The Girls Camp was considered more comfortable than the Boys Camp. On Sunday evening, everyone attended vesper services together on a grassy area at the edge of Lake Julia.

Summit Camps alumni still recall that camp was the best time of their lives, or at least their childhood. They created a Facebook page where memories and photos are posted. A typical comment echoes a popular sentiment: "Some of my fondest memories are from Summit Camp.…What I would give to go back one more summer. Simpler times for sure."

Lee Cone, a counselor in 1971, relates a story about the water tower. He and a friend stayed an extra week after the camp's final session was over. Ben Cart had hired them to paint the tower and close up the camp. They were given many gallons of an awful light-green color paint to use for the job. They painted the whole tower in a few days.

"It was just the two of us and a kitchen full of food. We had a great time and painted a huge peace symbol on top of the tower (in red paint, I think), which could only be seen from the air," Cone recalls. "Of course, there were no safety harnesses back in those days, just dumb college boys." Cone sums up the experience, "We lived though."

Jay Watson only went to Summit Camps for one year. It rained for his whole session. "Just miserable weather," Watson recalls. "No overnight hike. No sailing classes. Very little tennis." Because of the weather, he and his bunkmates spent a lot of time on the riflery range, which had a covered shooting area. He made it to Marksman First Class, a few good targets short of Sharpshooter. He remembers a dance at the Girls Camp in the dining hall:

> *There was square dancing and maybe regular dancing as well, at least the teenage version of it. I was quite the wallflower then, but the counselor and a couple of campers in our cabin convinced me that a cute girl across the way was looking over at me and wanted to dance. They managed to convince me to wander over, hands in pockets, and ask her to dance. Whereupon she promptly shot me down. She most certainly did not want to dance! I turned back around to see my counselor and bunkmates doubling over laughing. I could say it was mean, but it really was kind of funny.*

He and his parents traveled to Cedar Mountain from Athens, Georgia. On the way home, he got carsick (as he was prone to do) winding down US

The building for boys at Summit Camps is no longer standing. *Author's collection.*

276 to Greenville. "It was kind of the perfect finale after the underwhelming monsoon summer," Watson says.

The camp had a memorable Sadie Hawkins event where the girls had to catch the boys. The boys would have their ankles tied together. At a signal, the boys had to run or hop away from the girls. They always headed up a hill, figuring that girls would not want to make the climb. Still, the girls trekked up the incline and got their men.

Since Summit Camps was adjacent to the DuPont plant, campers could hear the horn blasting in the distance when there was a shift change. Summit Camps was similar to most other private camps of the era; it emphasized adventure, camaraderie and outdoor skills. What made it different was the proximity to the DuPont plant. The relationships between the two landowners were good. Campers and counselors could visit the waterfalls with just a phone call from the camp office. Before the covered bridge was built across the top of High Falls, campers held on to a chain to get to the other side. This was only a little safer than the way Ellen McCotter and her friends got over High Falls when they stayed at Buck Forest Lodge in the early 1950s. From the top, campers

The building for boys at Summit Camps has been taken down. *Author's collection.*

shimmied all the way down to the base of High Falls, something not allowed anymore. In the brochure from 1977, there's a photo of a group of girls hiking across the bottom of the second level of Triple Falls, which visitors can't do now.

AIRSTRIP TRAIL

The impact of the Summit Camps can be seen in several places in DuPont Forest. Visitors may just pass by a building and not question its origin, but an airstrip will get their attention. One of the many trails in the forest is called Airstrip Trail because that's what it was. The airstrip is still used under some circumstances.

Ben Cart was an active man. When he wasn't on site, he was busy promoting the camps by going to camping expositions and meeting with parents and prospective campers. He developed his passion for flying by getting his pilot license and buying a private plane. His obituary mentions

Airstrip Trail today. *Author's collection.*

that he flew many types of aircrafts, but his Focke-Wulf single-seater German plane was his favorite.

Since he spent so much time at Summit Camps, he decided to build an airstrip. Just like he built his camps, he enlisted his friends to help him. Ron Hubbard, owner of Hubbard Grading, and his crew oversaw the grading and leveling of the land. The airstrip measured 2,800 feet long and 40 feet wide.

One end of the airstrip offers great views of Mount Pisgah, probably the most recognized mountaintop in the area. Cart flattened both ends of the airstrip. On the Mount Pisgah side, he wanted to create a ski slope for his family in the winter. The idea was that one could ski from the airstrip down to the horse barn. That didn't work too well, according to some who tried or watched others attempt it. However, several adventurous camp counselors used the vertical drop for hang gliding.

The airstrip, completed in 1979, was only meant for private use. For several years, Cart and some parents flew in and out of Summit Camps. The camps operated from 1969 through 1985. When the camp closed, Cart sold all the land to the DuPont Corporation, but the sale was not finalized until 1991. DuPont executives and their successors used the airstrip to visit the site for meetings and recreation.

Since the land became part of DuPont Forest, the airstrip has been used for a variety of training exercises. The North Carolina Forest Service pilots practice their firefighting skills here. In case of a medical emergency, evacuation helicopters use the airstrip to transport patients.

BUCK FOREST DEVELOPMENT

Ben Cart's holdings were not confined to the Summit Camps. In the 1970s, Cart built a dam on the southern end of his property to create Buck Forest Lake, now known as Fawn Lake. This was a first step to designing and building Buck Forest Development. This housing estate would complement the airstrip and Summit Camps. Cart planned to market his development broadly, including camp alumni and parents of campers spending the summer at the Summit Camps.

But campers and this exclusive community would not rub elbows inadvertently. A new access from Reasonover Road to Buck Forest Drive was graded. He embellished the steep entranceway with several columns of decorative stone. The entry is now the current Fawn Lake Access Area, where the decorative stones provide an interesting anomaly in a state forest.

Ben Cart created a three-fold color brochure mailer to advertise his new venture. He was most likely going to send them to parents of current and past campers. Buck Forest was described as an "architecturally restricted private community of beautiful natural mountain homesites." A drawing shows a large one-family house, lots of floor-to-ceiling glass windows and a wraparound deck looking out into the void.

The private airport with its "paved and lighted runway" was highlighted. It was easily accessible by air—fifty minutes flight time from Atlanta or thirty minutes from Charlotte—presumably by private plane. From the brochure, it was clear that the residents of the Buck Forest property would have access to the amenities of Summit Camps, including Lake Julia.

Sherwood Forest and Connestee Falls, two major housing estates, were already operating in Cedar Mountain at the time. Other residential communities have peppered the area. The Buck Forest venture would be as successful as those other developments. Fawn Lake with its dock and gazebo and a decorative stone entrance to the Fawn Lake Access Area are all that remains of the Buck Forest idea. The houses and development never materialized, probably because Ben Cart was ready to take his life in another direction.

When DuPont Corporation managers were deciding if they should buy the Cart property, they realized that they had a problem with their current water system. After the federal Clean Water Act was amended in 1987, DuPont Corporation could no longer use the Little River for drinking water after heavy rains. The nitrate level in the Little River had increased because of heavier fertilizer use by farms, homes and even a golf course, resulting in blemishes in X-ray film. If the company bought the Summit Camps, it could use the water in Lake Julia when needed. By buying the Summit Camps property and the future housing development, it pushed out its environmental fence. Otherwise, who knows what new neighbors the company might get? In 1991, DuPont Corporation bought the property, including the camp buildings, Lake Julia and the airstrip.

Besides Lake Julia and Fawn Lake, visitors can see Ben Cart's legacy in DuPont Forest in buildings, an airstrip, a hangar, a horse barn and several cottages left standing. Ben Cart and his family loved DuPont Forest until he died in 2018. His obituary states, "In lieu of flowers, memorial contributions may be made to Friends of DuPont State Forest."

PART V
End of an Era

GROWING UP DUPONT

Growing up DuPont was a special experience. When you talk to DuPont kids today, you see the enthusiasm and love they had for their environment. Some are nostalgic for the long-gone days of swimming and playing in Lake DERA. Even those children who grew up before the lake was built remember the famous yearly picnics and the other children's events. Now, DuPont kids are not kids. Most are in their fifties, sixties or even seventies.

Connie Hubbard Corn is the daughter of Chan Hubbard, the first employee at the Brevard plant. She's in her fifties and a grandmother. Connie starts and ends talking about her father. "Chan never knew his dad. So, he didn't have role models. He had to figure out what dads should be like.…My dad truly loved his job—he truly loved and respected the property that is now DuPont Forest. He was once a keeper of the treasure that now thousands come enjoy." She has pictures of her dad with the kids and the jeep.

"The jeep is a vivid memory for us all," Connie recalls. "We spent a lot of time on the property in the jeep; for some odd reason, my best memory is running behind it. The pictures of Dad show him in his glory days. He was a strong man; he still is for his age."

"DuPont was the backdrop of my whole life," Connie says. "It was your job, your recreation, your life." Connie graduated from Brevard High and Blue Ridge Community College. She is now the marketing manager for the Self-Help Credit Union.

Her friends at school were like two tribes. Parents either worked for DuPont or the Ecusta paper mill. Both companies made huge contributions to the local schools. In the summer, DuPont families camped and hiked on the property along with church groups. They could bring Ecusta friends; in return, DuPont people could swim at Straus Park, owned by Ecusta.

"In the summer, we would go to work with our dad at DuPont. He'd drop us off at Lake DERA and pick us up at the end of the day," Connie says. "We also camped at High Falls where the shelter is now."

Connie's husband, David, is a plumber. His dad worked at Ecusta, the other tribe. Their first date was at High Falls; they married when she was twenty years old. Afterward, they camped on the DuPont property. Later, they gave their children the same opportunity.

But now Connie feels DuPont Forest is too crowded. She goes to Holmes Educational State Forest down the road, where it's a lot quieter. Her daughter owns a horse business and boards horses, so she benefits from DuPont Forest visitors. Her husband helps out the business with trail rides. "We still have the annual retired employees party," Connie says. "We're expecting over two hundred people this year."

Barbara Johnson Orr, Earle Johnson's eldest daughter, has different memories about DuPont than Connie, mostly because their age difference. Barbara is about fifteen years older than Connie.

Barbara and her family moved to Brevard when she was seven years old in 1957 and entered the third grade. She remembers that it was an all-White school then. Her Brevard elementary school was in an old school that no longer exists. The Johnsons lived right in town, and she was able to walk to school.

At the time, her high school had 75 percent Ecusta kids and 25 percent DuPont kids. After Brevard High School, she went to Western Carolina University and majored in business administration. In the summer, she worked at Rock Brook camp, running the children's bank. Barbara had been a Phi Mu sorority member, a large, respected fraternal organization. She went to work for Phi Mu in its Memphis, Tennessee office after graduation.

There were DuPont parties for adults. She watched as her parents got dressed up for a party at the Grove Park Inn in Asheville. But there weren't too many family activities on the DuPont property at the time. "The only interaction that I remember as a DuPont kid," Barbara says, "is the annual picnic." She was envious of the Ecusta kids who had Straus Park with a lake. She was able to go there to swim with friends. Since she was older than most DuPont children, she babysat for a lot of them.

"I don't remember going on the DuPont property for recreation. My dad was a big sightseer. We'd all pile in the car and go someplace on Sundays." When she was a child, they went to Pisgah Forest because it was closer. The family had a travel trailer, and they camped out.

She married a man she met in Memphis, and they moved to Jonesboro, Arkansas, where he grew up. She worked as an insurance adjuster. When her mother died in 2017, Barbara and her husband moved to Western North Carolina to be closer to her dad.

Brevard schools started integrating when she was in junior high school. "We didn't think about it too much. Blacks weren't 'run around friends.'" But there weren't any problems. She remembers that Brevard High School may have had less than 10 percent Black students at the time.

During her summer as a rising senior in high school, her dad managed to get two months off. The whole family—two adults, four children and a cousin from Massachusetts who was Barbara's age—piled into the station wagon, which pulled the trailer. The trailer had a shower and a toilet, but only her mom was allowed to use the trailer's toilet. The rest used the bathrooms in the campground.

"It was quite an adventure. We went to California, where I met my grandfather for the first and last time. We even went to Mexico….I couldn't afford it now with four kids. But with Uncle DuPont…that's what we called the company." This was her last hurrah before she went off to college. Barbara went to her twentieth and thirtieth high school reunions, but most friends have scattered. They no longer live in Brevard. She remembers Stuart English, who was in her high school class; unlike Barbara, he stayed and worked in Brevard.

Vicki Sprouse posted a blog about her memories as a kid at DuPont. In an excerpt from her blog, she writes:

> *I love summer…I really do…I think more now than I did when I was a kid. Now, I spend most of my summer days sitting in a work cubicle instead of out in the fresh air and sunshine, but I do try and find the time in the evening or on the weekends just to savor the season.*
>
> *When I was younger, summer was a magical time. While my mother didn't entertain me and my brother every single day…we were country*

kids and could entertain ourselves just fine thank-you-very-much…she ensured that we had lots of summer days full of good clean family fun.

In our hometown there were two major industries. My dad worked for DuPont. Back then I didn't think too much about the fact that the DuPont plant sat right smack dab in the middle of thousands of acres of private forest with trails, two rivers, waterfalls, camping, a lake, and a whole farm for the employees to enjoy. It was a normal thing for me.

As a kid I didn't realize that most companies didn't offer these amenities to their employees and how blessed we really were. Ecusta had a smaller version of what DuPont had, and it was called Camp Straus; it has since changed into an upscale residential development called Straus Park. That's where my husband's family hung out in the summers, because his parents worked for Ecusta. They always had a huge 4th of July picnic which most of the county attended, because nearly everyone in the county was a friend or family member of someone who worked at Ecusta.

Marty Griffin, now in his late sixties, has spent his whole life in Brevard. Marty's memories highlight his experiences as a summer hire. "My dad was the third employee at DuPont in Brevard." Bill, Marty's dad, had worked for a family grocery store before he moved to DuPont Corporation. Marty was in the first or second grade at the time. All new hourly employees got training in a building off site. Marty's father was a welder. But regardless of the new employee's skill set, DuPont Corporation focused its instruction on safety and cleanliness procedures.

"DuPont instilled the importance of safety on and off the job. If there was an accident in the home, that would cost time off the job as well. Injuries off the job were just as serious as injuries on the job," Marty says.

The company provided employees with steel-toed shoes and safety glasses. If workers needed prescription glasses, they got prescription safety glasses. The company helped the family with purchasing steel-toed shoes. "Also they emphasized cleanliness," Marty recalls. "The plant was cleaner than a hospital."

Marty went to Straus Elementary School, where Blue Ridge Community College is located now, then Brevard Junior High and High School. After the DuPont kids had one year of college, they were eligible for summer work. First Marty did maintenance work. There were always two people on the job, for safety reasons. Once he spent days just following an electrician around.

His most memorable job as a summer employee was riding with Charlie Paxton, the legendary DuPont Company forester. One day, Marty put his hand on a wooden fence and did not see the wasp nest underneath. He got stung but wanted to ignore it. "If you ignore it, we'll both get fired," Paxton said. They went to the company infirmary.

Marty also fed fish at Lake Dense. This way, clients who'd never fished before would be able to catch a fish. DuPont paid time and a half for overtime and double for holidays. In 1969, Marty made ten to twelve dollars an hour at DuPont. That's more than federal minimum wage now. "Citizen Telephone, the local telephone company owned by the Picklesimer family, had to raise their rates to keep up," Marty says.

Marty graduated from Mars Hill College and spent thirty-one years teaching social studies and coaching football. "You still see the DuPont family from the old days at funerals. DuPont and Ecusta weren't just places to work. They raised families."

DUPONT CORPORATION SELLS THE PLANT

In May 1995, DuPont Corporation announced that the Brevard plant was up for sale. This was the end of the DuPont manufacturing era in Western North Carolina. When Jamie Van Buskirk, an environmental engineer, came to work at the Brevard plant in 1995, employees told him, "You've come to close us down, haven't you?"

"When I first got to the site, DuPont was getting ready to sell the land," Van Buskirk said. Employees told him, "I know why you're here. I'm not worried about losing my job. I don't want to lose access to the land; we love the property."

In January 1996, DuPont Corporation sold more than 2,700 acres to Sterling Diagnostic Imaging, a financial investment acquisition firm that was going to continue manufacturing film, at least for a while. Sterling was to offer the same compensation and benefits as its predecessor to all its approximately two thousand employees. The company always believed that these were important factors that kept workers from wanting to join a union. According to former employees, everything stayed the same.

Sterling Diagnostic Imaging was a privately held company with major stock positions maintained by Sterling Group, the management of Sterling

Diagnostic, and its employees, as well as by several other investors, whose identities had not been publicly disclosed. Sterling Imaging signed a seven-year contract with Premier, the largest healthcare alliance in the United States, where under this agreement, Premier would buy all its medical films from Sterling.

But what was going to be the fate of the majority of the DuPont landholdings in Henderson and Transylvania Counties? As Chuck McGrady, a longtime environmentalist, former president of the Sierra Club and member of the North Carolina State House of Representatives, recalls, "Few people knew what was on the property, except some DuPont employees." Waterfalls and lakes seemed hidden behind corporate walls, although locals could always get permission to hike on the land.

As soon as DuPont Corporation announced that it was selling the plant and leaving the area, Jeff Jennings, an engineer with the company and an active environmentalist, met with Carolina Mountain Land Conservancy (CMLC) in Hendersonville. At the time, CMLC was a fledging land trust that had yet to complete its first conservation project. But this was the crucial meeting that led to more fruitful connections and relationships. Jennings explained that most of the acreage, bought in 1956 when land was so cheap, would be considered excess. It could be broken up and sold for development or even a landfill. What could the group do?

Although CMLC could not take on such a large project, McGrady, president of the land trust and a former Atlanta lawyer, had connections with The Conservation Fund. TCF, as it is known, was created out of The Nature Conservancy. Its mission is to work with local communities to protect land by helping to buy it quickly before the state is able to make this decision.

"The stars were aligned," McGrady says today about that era.

McGrady invited Rex Boner from the Atlanta TCF to listen to the DuPont land story. It was fortuitous that senior TCF already knew key people at DuPont Corporation at its headquarters in Wilmington, Delaware. The company at the time had a Land Legacy department that dealt with devolving land it no longer needed; it had disposed of land before at bargain prices. It worked with managers at the Brevard plant who had a better understanding of the land and the boundaries of the property. According to CMLC meeting minutes, it was also important to learn who the neighbors were around the property.

By October 1995, McGrady reported that the State of North Carolina had expressed an interest in acquiring the land as a state park. The negotiations were going well between TCF and the DuPont Corporation; it was a spectacular property with waterfalls and lakes. The company might make a final decision by the end of the year. CMLC's role was to provide local support and enable community leaders to understand this opportunity. They met with North Carolina General Assembly and North Carolina Senate representatives and tourist boards.

Things moved quickly. In less than a year, TCF did an appraisal of the DuPont property for tax purposes. It was clear that the state would only be interested in buying a contiguous piece of land. An interesting example involves nonadjacent land off Rich Mountain, above Camp High Rocks. Eventually, Camp High Rocks took possession of that land with a conservation easement, which means that it owns the land but cannot develop it.

By the beginning of 1997, DuPont Corporation had sold 7,600 acres to TCF for $2.2 million, considered a bargain sale. The tract included Stone Mountain, the highest point on the property, as well as three waterfalls: Hooker, Wintergreen and Grassy Creek. TCF transferred the land to the State of North Carolina. The funding came from the North Carolina Natural Heritage Trust Fund; this fund has now been folded into another agency and no longer exists by this name.

McGrady remembers that the DuPont Company was not demanding. It didn't require that the forest be named after the company. But it was felt that there were so many DuPont retirees and employees in the area that it was right to acknowledge them. Everyone felt very good when the company sold such a large tract of land for a nominal price.

But the land was not slated to become a state park. A North Carolina state park representative came from Raleigh to inspect the land and said, "We'll pass." At the same time, Gorges State Park in the southwestern part of the state was being created out of land formerly owned by Duke Energy. DuPont Forest became part of the North Carolina Forest Service.

"It was like a love fest. Hold hands and sing kumbaya," McGrady remembers. Retirees were supportive. It had been their playground. Now the land could be used for hunting and fishing as well. Saving the land would protect water quality. DuPont State Forest became a reality.

CMLC, the fledgling land trust that had made all the right connections, then turned its attention to small noncontiguous parcels that TCF had also bought from DuPont Corporation and wanted to sell. But the CMLC minutes of the December 1996 board meeting included a prophetic sentence:

> *Chuck McGrady further reported that it is expected that the Sterling property which included the 3 major waterfalls may be on the market in 5 or 6 years.*

The only thing wrong about McGrady's statement was the timing. It happened a lot more quickly.

HIKE: MIDSUMMER WALK FROM GUION FARM

For a small forest, DuPont has countless entrances and six access areas. This has a lot to do with its history—before, during the DuPont Corporation days and even later. Many trails start from a pull-off outside of the forest with a space or two for a vehicle.

The DuPont plant was located in Cedar Mountain, Transylvania County, but DuPont Corporation owned land in both Henderson and Transylvania Counties. Guion Farm is the main entrance on the northern side of the forest, which is very different from the High Falls area with its three waterfalls and Visitor Center. I turn off the main road—if Staton Road can be called a main road—and take Sky Valley Road. The road passes large homes, horse farms and houses under construction. At the intersection with Old CCC Road, the pavement stops. I pass the barred entrance to Buck Forest Road and then the Guion Farm Access Area. It's a huge parking lot, perfect for horse trailers and large vehicles. At 8:30 a.m. on a weekend morning, I'm the first one here.

On Tarklin Branch Road, the trail in front of the parking area, it's a hot summer scene with wide-leafed sunflowers swaying in the breeze. Pipsissewa (*Chimaphila maculata*), a short plant with thick leaves and drooping white flowers, hides among taller vegetation. Blackberries are still red and not yet ready for eating.

To hike all the trails in DuPont Forest, you have to walk many trails both ways—there and back. Many trails just don't connect to anything else. Other times, I need to redo a trail I've already walked to get to a new trail. When I hike in Great Smoky Mountains National Park, I use two or three trails in a day. But here, it could be a dozen trails, some both ways. So, to keep myself sane and on track, I create a spreadsheet of my planned hike. Here's the spreadsheet for this hike:

Guion Farm Hike

Trail	Miles	Next Turn	Comment
Park at Guion Farm			
Guion Farm Connector	0.2	Right on	
Tarklin Branch Road	1.0	Right on	
Tarklin Branch Road	0.6	Right on	There and back
Sandy Trail	0.5	Right on	
Grassy Creek Trail	2.2	Right on	There and back
Sandy Trail	0.1	Right on	
Wintergreen Falls Trail	0.2	Right on	There and back
Wintergreen Falls Trail	0.4	Right on	
Tarklin Branch Road	0.9	Right on	
Shoal Creek Trail	0.4	Left on	There and back
Walk on SR 1128	??	Right on	
Farmhouse Trail	1.2	Right on	There and back
Guion Farm Connector	0.2	Left on	
Buck Forest Road	0.3	Right on	
White Pine Trail	0.5	Right on	
Hickory Mountain Road	0.3	Right on	
Guion Farm Connector	0.2		
Drive north to Guion Trail			
Guion Trail	0.4		There and back
Total	**9.6**		
Sky Valley Road continues			
I could pick up Flat Rock Trail	1.0		There and back

On Sandy Trail, two mountain bikers come toward me. I move to the right as far as I can.

"Hiker up," the first one says.

"Are you the last one?" I ask the second cyclist.

"Yep," he replies. Both parties speak their lines as expected. I wish all cyclists were as knowledgeable as them. Multi-use trails work when we're all trained. Bikers are supposed to yield to hikers—some say "every single time," but the reality is that bikers are faster, bigger and have a harder time stopping than I do.

Grassy Creek Trail is new to me. I have to rock hop across the creek. The stepping stones are flat and reasonably close together, but I lose my nerve partway through and just walk through the water. My feet will be wet all day, but I feel safer. Now the trail is rocky and rough.

Guion Farm was once a farm. It's now thickly wooded, except for a cleared area around the parking lot. A *Hendersonville Heritage* article explains:

> *The DuPont Corp. established a forest management program under the leadership of Charles Paxton. One of the first forest practices was the establishment of 330 acres of white pines on abandoned pastureland in the area known as the Flatwoods or Guion Farm. In 1957 the DuPont Corp. entered into an agreement with Champion Paper to harvest timber from other areas of the property. Many harvested areas were re-planted with white pine.*

By the time Paxton retired in 1978, he had planted two million white pines.

Then to Wintergreen Falls, a waterfall that's considered off the beaten path. Still, when I get there about 11:00 a.m., there are plenty of bikers and one hiker with a dog on a leash. "Thank you for keeping your dog on a leash," I say.

Wintergreen is named after the wintergreen or teaberry, a ground cover around the falls. The water only drops a modest twenty feet. It attracts fewer people than the three falls on the Visitor Center side of the forest. To see the falls, you have to scramble up rocks and roots. It's hidden behind trees and shrubs all the while you're climbing; you need to have faith that it will be there. Then the shrubbery clears and you're facing the chute square on. No signs warn visitors to keep off the rocks, although you shouldn't climb up any waterfall.

I retrace my steps back on Tarklin Branch Road. When I round the corner, I hear a woman's voice. "Now wait you guys"—obviously speaking to children tearing up the trail on their bikes. Then there's a loud "Danny!"

It's Sara Landry with her son, Zac, and his friend. Landry is the executive director of Friends of DuPont. We talk about the upcoming DuPont Forest master plan—or, to be more exact, future funding for the future master plan.

End of an Era

Sara Landry, executive director of Friends of DuPont Forest, riding in the forest. *Author's collection.*

The forest has been growing with donations of small parcels of land here and there, which have been gratefully accepted. But now the forest needs to have a plan to integrate these new pieces.

The last few trails are a mystery. I can't find them on the ground as easily as I did on the map. "Don't confuse the map with the territory," one of my teachers used to say. I don't exactly know what the context was, but the sentiment is correct.

I deviate from my carefully constructed spreadsheet and find Shoal Creek Trail last. It's a dark, shady trail where mushrooms have popped up. I grab Shoal Creek Trail as well as Farmhouse Trail and walk back to my car. The whole hike is 9.6 miles in about four and a half hours, including lunch. That was the easy part.

I drive up Sky Valley Road to look for Flat Rock Trail, as my notes state, but the road gets rougher and rougher. I worry about getting stuck on the road, and I can't find the trailhead. I'll have to leave it for another visit. So far, I've walked fifty-four distinct miles out of the one hundred miles in the forest. Plenty more to go.

FIGHT FOR THE FALLS

Sterling Diagnostic was never slated to stay long at the Brevard plant. On February 1, 1999, Sterling Diagnostic Imaging sold the film plant to Agfa, a company based in Belgium. The new owners bought only about 476 acres, just what they felt they needed to continue manufacturing film.

The rest of the land, 2,223 acres, was known as the "waterfall tract" because it held three major waterfalls—Triple, Bridal and High Falls. The tract also included Lakes Julia, Dense, Alford and the airstrip that Ben Cart had built for his summer camp.

The waterfall tract was owned by the Sterling Group, a group of Texas investors. They decided to sell the land to Waterfall Investment Group LLC, a company owned by Jim Anthony. Anthony, a real estate developer, planned to build the Cliffs at Brevard, an upscale housing estate.

Anthony bought the highly desirable property for $6.35 million in a one-shot, closed-bid sale. A former lineman for the local telephone company, he had already built several exclusive residential communities. The waterfall tract was perfect for his next project. The developer immediately began road construction.

The State of North Carolina, with the help of The Conservation Fund, bid $5.5 million. It's still unclear why the owners would sell the land without giving the state a chance to make a counteroffer.

At first, Anthony said that he planned to use the land as a private retreat. The land deed stated that the property could not be used for residential purposes. He could not build houses but could use it for "private recreational uses such as fishing, hiking, hunting, boating, camping and private cabin lodging." What was private cabin lodging? And was the housing ban enforceable? At this time, he had not sold any home sites but had sold lots in his South Carolina development with the promise that property owners could go up to Brevard and enjoy the waterfalls.

By the end of 1999, Anthony declared that he was going to build houses on the

"No Trespassing" sign put up while a developer temporarily owned land in DuPont Forest. *Author's collection.*

property after all. This would provide jobs to the building trade in the area. Locals who knew the beauty and value of the waterfalls were appalled. Many forces came together to make sure the land was saved for the public.

At the time, Chet Meinzer, the DuPont property manager, told Anthony that the plant was still operating and that there was always the possibility of chemical leakage and emergency procedures. "It didn't seem to faze Anthony," Meinzer remembers. Maybe Anthony didn't fully appreciate the potential problems of putting high-value homes next to a working chemical plant.

At this point, savvy locals understood what was happening: Anthony was going to build houses. DuPont employees already knew about the beauty of the waterfalls. They and their families had been able to hike and camp on the land. When DuPont Forest was created, it quickly became popular with hikers, bikers and equestrians. People outside the area only knew about the waterfalls from the 1992 movie *The Last of the Mohicans*. At this time, there were no North Carolina Forest Service personnel on site. The forest was managed from Asheville by John Pearson, regional forester, and his assistant forester, Ed Goforth.

People in Transylvania and Henderson Counties mounted a campaign to encourage the state to buy the land from Anthony. Jim Hunt was the governor of North Carolina at the time, the longest-serving governor in the history of the state. He was in office for eight years from 1977 to 1985 and again from 1993 to 2001. The year, 2000, was an election year, and that helped the waterfall cause. Some Democratic politicians from Eastern North Carolina were looking to promote an issue in the western part of the state—saving the waterfalls seemed like a good one.

Chuck McGrady, a former national Sierra Club president and a Republican state representative who helped save the first land acquisition, worked with Sam Neill, a Hendersonville attorney, to come up with a compromise. They thought that Anthony could build homes on most of his property. But at least McGrady thought the area around the waterfalls would be included in the state forest. Alan Hirsch, deputy attorney general for the state, explored every possible step short of condemning the land.

Both McGrady and Neill were well connected in the state. Neill met with legislators in Raleigh to show them maps and photographs of the property. He talked about the compromise. All were astonished when the governor and other elected officials spoke in favor of taking the whole property. "I was never told before this that I wasn't thinking big enough," McGrady says. "But that's what the governor told me."

DuPont Forest

By then, a core group of farsighted locals formed a group that advocated for saving the whole property. Jeff Jennings, the DuPont plant employee who helped the company sell the first parcel of land to the state, nature lover Aleen Steinberg and equestrian Gwen Hill were already on the DuPont State Forest Advisory Committee. They and other activists created Friends of the Falls in April 2000. Emotions ran high as they worked to move public sentiments. These leaders felt that they were going to be more excluded from these cherished waterfalls than when DuPont Corporation owned the land.

For a brief while, this issue made national news, as the *New York Times* and *Baltimore Sun* covered the dispute. Forest activists wrote articles and letters to the newspapers. They emailed their legislators and instructed others to do the same. Friends of the Falls put an advertisement in the *Henderson Times-News* encouraging readers to mail this ad to Governor Hunt. A map of DuPont Forest was included that showed the affected area right in the middle of the forest. The ad said:

> *We have a unique opportunity to protect and make available to everyone these natural wonders.*
>
> *Do we want to lose these world-class waterfalls?...*
>
> *If you want these falls added to the heart of DuPont State Forest, tell Government Jim Hunt.*

Ken Shelton wrote an op-ed in *Henderson Times-News* dated March 26, 2000, encouraging readers to write to the North Carolina Council of State. Shelton, a radiologist at a local hospital, described himself as an avid mountain biker and outdoor enthusiast. What was notable about this op-ed was that Shelton listed every member of the Council of State along with their contact information, including their email address. The Council of State comprises the senior state government officials, including the lieutenant governor, the agriculture secretary and the state treasurer.

And people listened. Those who sent cards, letters and emails received a letter from Mike Easley, the attorney general at the time, dated November 1, 2000, concerning the fate of the three waterfalls:

> *The Council of State voted to acquire the forest property that had been slated for development. The action followed many long months of negotiations by*

my lawyers, who had the difficult task of fully exploring whether a voluntary agreement could ever be reached to achieve the State's goals of adequately protecting water quality and preserving the watershed and waterfalls for the people.... The State's only choice was to acquire the threatened property by the power of eminent domain and thus make the DuPont Forest whole.

Property rights advocates also mounted their fight, denouncing condemnation of the land as abuse of power. Even Horace Jarrett, chair of the Transylvania County Board of Commission, opposed state ownership. Many locals anticipated construction jobs in Anthony's housing plans. Transylvania County said that it needed the extra property taxes.

The state took title by eminent domain to 2,223 acres on October 24, 2000, after top officials making up the North Carolina Council of State voted the day before. Then there was the matter of the price. Jim Anthony had paid $6.35 million. He said that he had made major improvements totaling in the millions. The state paid the developer $24 million, almost four times the price. Anthony built the covered bridge at the top of High Falls and a second bridge on Conservation Road at the outflow of Lake Julia. He built a road to Bridal Veil Falls from Conservation Road. The North Carolina Forest Service then added the circle to build the trail to the falls. The current Visitor Center was going to be the sales office for the housing development. It was partially built when the state acquired the waterfalls tract. But the public had an intact forest—well, not quite. Agfa was still operating on 476 acres, in what has become known as the "donut hole."

In 2001, the North Carolina Wildlife Federation, in cooperation with the National Wildlife Federation, chose Friends of the Falls to receive the Governor's Award as Conservationist of the Year. This honor came in recognition of the Friends' efforts in saving this land from commercial development. Friends of the Falls disbanded by donating its remaining funds and much of its leadership talent to a new organization, Friends of DuPont Forest.

ALAN HIRSCH REMEMBERS THE FIGHT FOR THE WATERFALLS

In 2000, Alan Hirsch was the deputy attorney general working under Attorney General Mike Easley. Hirsch worked to acquire the tract with three major waterfalls.

When Jim Anthony announced that he was going to build houses on the land surrounding the waterfalls, he created a brochure. One day, Mike Easley called Hirsch into his office and showed him the brochure. "Go save the land," Easley said.

Hirsch had no idea what he was talking about, but he quickly learned the story. He called Jim Anthony and said, "We need to talk." This started several months of conversation between Hirsch, Anthony and Anthony's lawyers.

Anthony was already discussing public access with the Department of Natural Resources (DENR). At the time, DENR was responsible for the North Carolina Division of Parks and Recreation; since then, DENR has been reorganized into the Department of Environmental Quality (DEQ). Under the agreement, the public would be able to see the waterfalls from a narrow corridor but had to stay in that corridor. They could see the falls but would also see the residential community.

But Hirsch wanted the public to have full access. He worked with Jim Anthony for several months, but they made little progress. Hirsch saw the importance of total access. He recalls that Anthony was very resistant. Attorney General Easley wanted him to take the land. "Fix it," Easley said.

DENR was trying to negotiate an agreement that was much more favorable to Jim Anthony. DENR and Hirsch went to Governor Jim Hunt to try to resolve their internal differences. Hirsch remembers going into the study on the first floor of the Governor's Mansion. They spread out the maps on a large circular table. Governor Hunt was not aware of the issue at this point. DENR and Hirsch each made their case on how to handle the land and save the waterfalls.

Governor Hunt looked at the maps and saw the importance of the land immediately. "This is what the people of North Carolina will have forever," Hunt said. The governor looked at the big picture. The issue was now back in Hirsch's court. The governor's wishes did not automatically translate to eminent domain, but that was the backup plan.

In the meantime, Hirsch was talking to Jeff Jennings once a week. Jennings, still working at the Brevard plant, kept him abreast of what was going on the ground on the DuPont land. Anthony kept saying that he's ready to build. "If you build, the negotiations are off. I'm going to take the land," Hirsch tell him.

Each week, Hirsch would say, "I'm going to take the land." Anthony didn't believe it. They were getting nowhere. It was a staring contest. Who was going to blink first? Anthony's lawyers started calling Hirsch.

"I will talk until you start building," Hirsch said. "Then I will have no choice but to take the land." They repeated themselves week after week. They tried to get an agreement where Anthony would have a much smaller development.

One Monday morning, Jeff Jennings called Hirsch. "The bulldozers are moving and they're taking down trees." Hirsch called Anthony's lawyers: "We're going to take the land." But Anthony didn't offer to remove the bulldozers. Hirsch assumed that Anthony knew that people on the ground were keeping him appraised of the situation.

Just by coincidence, the Council of States was meeting the next day. Hirsch went to Governor Hunt to explain the story. "Go ahead and talk to the Council of States," the governor said, even though the issue was not on the agenda. Alan Hirsch made the presentation, explaining the whole story right up to and including the bulldozers on the land.

The Council of States meetings are public, so anyone can come and listen. Anthony's lawyers spoke as well. Easley made a motion to take the land. The governor said he supported the attorney general's position. The Council of States took a vote, and it was unanimous for acquiring the land. Within days, the state owned the land, and Anthony had to stop bulldozing and remove his equipment. Once it happened, it went fast. Then Anthony and the state started the negotiations over the price.

Hirsch had not seen the land in person while he worked on this issue. About five years ago, he and his daughter went down to DuPont Forest. Jeff Jennings organized someone to guide them around the waterfalls that Hirsch had helped save. When Mike Easley became governor in the year 2000, Alan Hirsch went to work for him as a policy adviser. "Now I do healthcare work. I've been a do-gooder all my life," he says.

ALEEN STEINBERG, ENVIRONMENTAL ACTIVIST

Aleen Steinberg first learned about Western North Carolina when her daughter was in summer camp in Arden, about twenty miles north of DuPont Forest. Originally from Baraboo, Wisconsin, she's lived in Transylvania County for fifty-five years, thirty of them part time.

Her main residence was in Tampa, which she shared with her husband, Bill Steinberg, many years her senior. When she came to pick up her

Aleen Steinberg, environmental activist. *Author's collection.*

daughter from camp, she was sold on the area. She now lives in a dream house that she built on ten acres on top of a hill in a Cedar Mountain development, with a guest house, a gazebo and landscaped grounds. Her huge kitchen was designed to remind her of her German immigrant grandmother, complete with baskets and bottles on the walls.

As a child growing up in Wisconsin, Steinberg loved the outdoors and hiking. Aldo Leopold (1887–1948), the famous conservationist and ecologist, lived ten miles from her grandparents' home. Earlier, John Muir had emigrated from Scotland to Central Wisconsin when he was eleven. Although Muir is best known for his writing about the Sierras, he got his love for the outdoors in Wisconsin. In *The Story of My Boyhood and Youth*, he wrote, "Oh, that glorious Wisconsin wilderness!"

In Tampa, Steinberg was involved in mental health concerns, on the hospital board and an activist for children. In 1968, she attended the Conference on Children. She was also an environmental activist, both in Tampa and in Cedar Mountain as a member of the Sierra Club. The DuPont Corporation allowed non-employees to explore its property with the proper permission. Steinberg led hikes on DuPont land before it was public, starting in about 1964. She remembers that her groups included Cedar Mountain people, summer people and teenagers. Early on, she understood the unique features of the DuPont Corporation land. "Lucky. Aren't we lucky?" she says.

Steinberg was on the advisory board as well as a representative for the Sierra Club for the first piece of DuPont land that the State of North Carolina bought in 1997. "I was surprised when DuPont sold the land to the state," Steinberg says. "After that, the public could visit Wintergreen and Hooker Falls." Steinberg wrote a grant to build the observation tower, which would be wheelchair accessible. National Sierra Club gave them $5,000.

In 1999, Steinberg recalls when the developer Jim Anthony first said that the land that he had bought from Sterling was for recreation by owners of his other properties. Then it was going to be cabins. Cabins morphed into houses. "It was obvious that it was going to be a gated community." The public was "going to be able to go to an observation tower and look at the falls." The rallying cry was, "The waterfalls belong to everyone."

Jeff Jennings, who still worked for Agfa, and Steinberg tried to figure out what to do. They discussed saving the waterfalls as they hiked. Jennings said, "We have to create a 501(c)(3)." The group became Friends of the Falls in the year 2000.

Dr. Ken Shelton, a radiologist, held a meeting in the Hendersonville library. A bearded man spoke in favor of saving the land. "If a bearded Republican wants this, it could work," Steinberg thought. But there was opposition to the condemnation from other locals who saw jobs in the building trade.

More meetings were held in the Cedar Mountain Community Center. It was packed with silver seniors and young bikers, as Steinberg describes them. The group sent four thousand emails and letters to Governor Hunt. "We just kept at it." The Friends of the Falls met every Monday evening at Steinberg's house—about twenty-two Friends of Falls members.

In October 2000, they heard that the land had been taken from the developer by eminent domain. It was wonderful. She quoted Margaret

Aleen Steinberg Visitor Center in DuPont Forest. *Author's collection.*

Mead: "Never doubt that a small group of thoughtful, committed citizens can change the world; indeed, it's the only thing that ever has."

She's seen lots of changes in the area over the years. When she first came to the area, Brevard College was a junior college. There were a few mom and pop restaurants in the area. She remembers that the current Cedar Mountain Café opposite the fire station had been Grammy's, a hamburger joint, and an antique store before that. "The closest ABC store was in Hendersonville. Eventually, there was a vote to be able to serve alcohol in Transylvania County. It was a very divisive and controversial issue."

Steinberg has two children. Her daughter, who lives in Fort Lauderdale, also has a house close by in Cedar Mountain. She lives locally about five months out of the year.

After the waterfalls were saved, Steinberg continued her involvement with the forest. She was on the board of Friends of DuPont for twelve years, with a break in between. She was on the DuPont State Forest Advisory Committee and worked on the Junior Ranger program for DuPont Forest, now a reality.

The Aleen Steinberg Visitor Center opened in 2013. "I have no idea how it happened. Someone wanted to honor me. It came as a surprise," Steinberg says. "It's very humbling." The 2,600-square-foot center is located in a handcrafted log building that once was slated to serve as a sales office for the defunct development.

Steinberg just turned ninety years old. She keeps plugging on, taking daily walks. She likes to walk to Fawn Lake and back. Her favorite falls is Wintergreen. She still goes to High Falls. "The joy is in the journey."

FAUNA AND FLORA IN THE FOREST

With all this human history, we might be forgiven if we forget that DuPont Forest is, first and foremost, a forest with plants and animals. People have spotted bears, skunks, opossums, turtles, otters and many amphibians. DuPont Forest has most of the same animals that populates the rest of Southern Appalachia. The wildlife is not going to be obvious. With so much activity on the trail—hiking, biking, dogs, trail running—visitors are not going to meet a bear as they turn a corner. That's true of most forests; you have to be quiet, still and probably by yourself. You also have to be lucky.

End of an Era

Two mammals stand out because, like so many people in the Southern Appalachians, they're also transplants: coyotes and wild boars.

Coyotes have been called one of the most adaptable animals. Wile E. Coyote and the Road Runner are a duo from the *Looney Tunes* cartoons. In every episode, the Coyote tries to catch the Road Runner with Rube Goldberg maneuvers and equipment. But, of course, the bird always escapes. In reality, coyotes are quite intelligent and survivalists. They are indigenous to North America and came originally from the prairies and desert areas. Wolves used to be their main predators. As humans have killed off wolves, coyotes have moved east and even into cities. They're filling the role of large predators without any real enemies. The species is versatile, able to adapt to and expand into environments modified by humans.

Coyotes look like large dogs. They're nocturnal, and visitors are most likely to see them at dusk. They eat rodents and small mammals but are known as opportunistic eaters—they'll eat anything. Some land managers, like Great Smoky Mountains National Park, consider coyotes a protected species because they traveled here on their own. The North Carolina Wildlife Commission lists them as an invasive species and has a hunting season for coyotes. DuPont Forest follows the guidelines of the North Carolina Wildlife Commission. Armadillos have already migrated north and have been seen in the Smokies. When will they show up in DuPont Forest?

Wild boars, however, did not move here on their own. They were transported to Western North Carolina from Europe by Gordon Moore, an adviser to English investors, who wanted to establish a game preserve. The lodge and hunting lands were located near Robbinsville in Graham County. Beginning in 1912, they imported buffalo, elk, mule deer, Russian brown bears and wild boars.

The boars were the only animals that escaped and survived in the wild. They made themselves at home in the Southern Appalachian and spread in all directions. To make matter worse, they can breed year-round and have up to twelve piglets at a time. Boars dig up the soil searching for roots and leave the ground looking like it's been rototilled.

"They especially love the tubers of the showy spring species: bloodroot, trillium, rue anemone, blue cohosh, trout lily, etc." explains George Ellison, author and naturalist. Ellison's property abuts Great Smoky Mountains National Park and is visited by wild boars when their house is empty for a while.

DuPont Forest

Of the sixty-six species of salamanders found in North Carolina, the green salamander (*Aneides aeneus*) was the only amphibian listed as endangered by the state. But recently, they've been reclassified as a threatened species of native salamanders; the label "threatened" is one step less dire than "endangered." The salamanders hide in crevices of rock outcroppings. They're dark green with yellow splotches and resemble lichen, so they're not easy to spot. Unless you go with an experienced naturalist, you may never see these elusive creatures.

Blue ghost fireflies are native to DuPont Forest and now a well-documented part of the forest. That doesn't mean that many people have seen them. To experience their blue glow, you need to be in the right place at the right time with the right weather conditions. The blue ghosts glow as part of a mating ritual from mid-May to mid-June.

Blue ghosts need undisturbed, cool, moist conditions, which can certainly be found in the forest. They live in damp leaf litter. During mating season, the male flitters about two to three feet off the ground looking for mates. The females are wingless; they glow and wait for their man. Because the females can't fly, this species of fireflies doesn't move around much. They're a vulnerable population. Several years ago, Friends of DuPont Forest took visitors on short hikes to view this phenomenon but now has suspended these events. The North Carolina Forest Service closes several trails for a few weeks to give the blue ghosts privacy and chance to reproduce.

Kids in the South call all fireflies "lightning bugs" and try to catch them and keep them in a glass jar. These soft-bodied beetles light up during twilight to attract mates or prey. Blue ghosts may not be as well-known as their cousins, the synchronous firefly (*Photuris frontalis*). The latter are famous for blinking on and off in a mating ritual. In Great Smoky Mountains National Parks, the rangers created an elaborate lottery system and offer bus transportation to the site for visitors to experience the synchronous fireflies. At DuPont Forest, it's a little quieter.

Most forest lovers get out in the spring to see the first wildflowers of the season. About 150 wildflowers have been identified at DuPont Forest. Mountain laurel, rhododendrons and flame azaleas are magnificent when they bloom close together. But flowers in the summer and autumn also require our attention and enthusiasm. Yellow-fringed orchids can be seen in the summer on the roadside.

Hearts-a-Bustin' (*Euonymus americanus*) is the nom de plume for the strawberry bush. A quiet, inconspicuous bush most of the year, the fruit bursts into flame in the fall. A rough shell holds the fruit, which turns bright pink, resembling a strawberry. As autumn progresses, the shell splits and bursts open to reveal intensely red berries. That's when most people notice the plant and pull out their cameras.

JEFF JENNINGS SAVES A FOREST

If anyone has had a pivotal effect on saving DuPont Forest, it is Jeff Jennings. He has been on the ground for both acquisitions of DuPont Forest land. A former DuPont Corporation employee, he was too young to retire when the last owner, Agfa, closed its doors in 2002. Jennings, now fifty-eight years old, exudes an athleticism and agility of a much younger person.

Jennings grew up in both North and South Carolina in an evangelical family. He went to high school in a small town in Upstate South Carolina and graduated as a mechanical engineer from Clemson University, located only fifty miles south of DuPont Forest.

He started work at DuPont Corporation in 1985. Like several other engineers on the site, he was hired into a prestigious rotation program where he was assigned to various locations through several DuPont departments. The job took him to South Carolina; Tennessee; the company headquarters in Wilmington, Delaware; and lastly to Western North Carolina.

When Jennings arrived from Wilmington, Delaware, in 1991, he promptly fell in love with the area. "I was stunned by the beauty of the place," he says. The blizzard of 1993 did not dampen his enthusiasm for the area.

"What did you move here for? They're going to close the place down," he recalls some of his new coworkers saying. There were already rumors that the plant was short-lived because of the impact of digital films on X-ray film production.

Jennings was sent on a business trip to Germany for several weeks, and he came back an environmentalist. He was going to learn every trail in Pisgah National Forest. "I think the biggest impact was that in Germany, they had better access to nature with greenways and bike paths. They had more than ten times the number of trails compared to our population density. People were healthier and happier living in walkable communities. They had a high priority on recycling, energy conservation and quality of life through free time in nature. I came to see our lack of public access for walking and biking as a type of poverty, even if we didn't recognize it as such."

"The DuPont property was first and foremost for the customers and then for the employees," Jennings recalls. Radiologists came to fish for trout in the stocked lakes and then grilled them at Triple Falls shelter. DuPont's main product was X-ray film, mostly for medical uses and then some industrial non-destructive B&W film. When radiologists and hospital staff visited the Brevard plant from all over the country, they would be entertained by the staff and taken to the waterfalls. They could stay overnight at various places, such as the Guion Farmhouses, the house on Sky Valley Road or at times on the former Summit Camps property. The lakes were aggressively stocked with trout. Customers would fish and then enjoy fried trout and steaks on the grill afterward. The company saw the lakes as a powerful draw to increase sales of X-ray film.

In 1995, DuPont Corporation announced that it was selling the plant because digital film was coming along. There were rumors that the land would be used for real estate and a landfill. "You always want to place your landfill at the edge of the county." Jennings was heartbroken.

A year before, Jennings had been the president of Environmental and Conservation Organization (ECO), an environmental organization in Henderson County; ECO has now merged with other advocacy groups to become MountainTrue. After the DuPont Corporation announcement, he called the Land Legacy department at DuPont headquarters in Wilmington. The Land Legacy group gives away or sells land cheaply to protect it from development. The Brevard plant was not the first time that the company had disposed of unneeded land this way.

Jennings also went to a board meeting of the nonprofit Carolina Mountain Land Conservancy (CMLC), now Conserving Carolina, to explain the situation. Chuck McGrady, then its president, had good connections with The Conservation Fund, a national conservation funding agency that buys up land quickly and resells it to a government entity. "It's all about initial connections between groups and people," Jennings says.

The original tract of land that became public in 1997 included Hooker Falls, Grassy Creek Falls and Wintergreen. Jennings named Wintergreen Falls because it's surrounded by teaberry, also known as wintergreen.

"Only a couple of years later," Jennings says, "Sterling Diagnostics sold 2,223 acres of land in a private sale to Jim Anthony, the property developer. In most cases, you always give the state the right of last refusal, so that the state knows what the land is worth. But they didn't do that in this case."

This whole negotiation was awkward for Jennings at work because people knew that he was working with the state to save the land from development.

Some, especially in Transylvania County, were against the condemnation because they saw the potential of construction jobs in the planned upscale housing. By the time the state condemned the land originally bought by a developer, Agfa was operating the plant. Jennings left the company as a senior process development engineer only six months before the plant shut down.

"Some professionals left the area after 2002 because they were too young to retire," Jennings says. Hourly workers stayed here because they came from this area, but they were never able to duplicate their salaries. Most professionals also stayed and retired in the area. Some bridged their salary with a home business. People loved living here. It was a low-cost area.

Jennings was one former employee who loved living here. In 2002, he wasn't even forty years old. As a mechanical engineer, one of his area of specialty was fluid delivery systems. For example, in creating film, various fluids, like coating emulsion, have to flow to the right heads. Jennings used his expertise to start Equilibar, a company north of Hendersonville that specializes in designing and manufacturing patented fluid control valves and back pressure regulators for research and industry. Equilibar may be considered a small business because it has fewer than thirty employees. But the company recently received the 2019 President's Award for Exports.

Jennings continues to advocate for the long-term viability of DuPont Forest; he was president of Friends of DuPont Forest for several years and is on the DuPont State Forest Advisory Committee. He still mountain bikes and hikes in the same forest where he worked decades ago.

THE X-RAY PLANT CLOSES

By 1999, Agfa had bought the film plant. While Sterling Diagnostic Imaging was an investment company based in Texas, Agfa is a Belgium company with long roots in film production. For the most part, DuPont Forest and Agfa, in the center of the forest, were good neighbors. The plant always had a separate entrance, which was gated and controlled. But the boundaries between public and private weren't always perfect. The roads and trails inside the forest had been laid out and built when DuPont Corporation was the overseer of more than ten thousand acres.

In early 2002, Agfa closed a short section of Conservation Road that veered onto its property. Located below the Lake Julia Dam, this closed piece

Agfa was the last owner of the original DuPont Corporation plant in Brevard. *Courtesy of the Rowell Bosse North Carolina Room, Transylvania County Library.*

connects two major visitor sights from the High Falls area to Bridal Veil Falls. Agfa requested that the forest service make it clear with signs and gates that this was private property.

Agfa cited liability concerns. "If someone were to get hurt, then we would be sued," an Agfa manager is quoted as saying. Experienced and hardy forest users who studied a map could take other trails that went around the closed sections. But most visitors had to decide if they wanted to see the two major falls—High and Triple on Staton Road—or go south to Reasonover Road to enjoy Bridal Veil Falls.

But bigger issues loomed. Soon after the closure of a small section of Conservation Road, Agfa announced that the company would be closing the Brevard plant by the end of 2002. At this point, it only employed 400 workers from a high of 1,500. They were well-compensated employees, as it was always emphasized. Agfa was not pulling out of the film production business; it was consolidating its operations in Bushy Park, South Carolina, north of Charleston.

Pensions and benefits were offered to all eligible employees with various combinations of ages and years of service. At the time, more than half of the employees lived in Transylvania County, about 40 percent were from

Henderson County and the remainder commuting from mostly Asheville and Greenville. Many employees needed to find new work or start businesses of their own. This was an economic blow to Transylvania County. The Ecusta Company, just up the road and in the same county, had been sold to a private owner who closed the plant down the same year.

But DuPont/Sterling/Agfa employees were resilient. Some had already left and taken other jobs. In the months between the announcement and the closing at the end of 2002, many made plans. Some had found jobs as technicians in other facilities. Those with scientific backgrounds retrained as math and science teachers. Some women took this opportunity to go to community college. It was also a chance to start or focus on businesses such as landscaping that catered to the affluent summer and second home market.

But it wasn't easy; the country was recovering from the 2001 dot-com bubble and recession. At the national level, the jobless rate rose by 1.1 percentage points to 5.8 percent in 2002. Many employees started at DuPont Corporation after high school and thought they would stay here until they retired. They never regained the salaries and benefits they had with their large companies.

A few employees were able to transfer to Agfa's administrative office in Greenville or move to the manufacturing plant in Bushy Park. Chuck Ramsey, a mechanical engineer, moved to Bushy Park with Agfa.

"My wife and I knew that this move to South Carolina wasn't permanent, so we never sold our house in Transylvania County. We treated living close to Charleston as an opportunity, like a vacation." They visited sites as tourists. After Ramsey and his wife moved back to North Carolina in 2006, he worked as a professional trail builder. He's always been an avid mountain biker. If bikes had license plates, he would be biker #001. Ramsey continues to bike and is active in the Friends of DuPont Forest group.

Agfa employees worked diligently until November 2002, when the American flag came down for the last time. But as the saying goes, it's not over until it's over. Although the plant had multiple owners, the cleanup rights and responsibilities reverted back to DuPont Corporation. As part of an agreement, Agfa had to take down the buildings. Then DuPont Corporation would come back to clean up the site.

PART VI
The Forest Grows Up

DAVE BROWN, FIRST FOREST SUPERVISOR

By 1997, DuPont State Forest was a reality; 7,600 acres of dirt roads, trails, three waterfalls and several lakes. Little by little, visitors discovered the wonders of the forest by walking, mountain biking and riding horses. The land could be described as a large donut with a hole of private land in the middle where Sterling Imaging continued to make film. Fences made the boundaries between public and private very clear.

The forest was technically under the supervision of the Asheville District of the North Carolina Forest Service. In reality, volunteers took on the informal role of keeping an eye on the forest and the visitors. No one is remembered as well as Bill Devendorf, a full-time volunteer caretaker. He drove his pickup truck around the property, answered visitors' questions, gave them maps and dealt with emergencies. He also coordinated the work for visiting forest rangers from other locations.

Devendorf came to DuPont Forest after a full career. He started in the 1930s with the Civilian Conservation Corps in Pisgah National Forest. He joined the army—serving in World War II, Korea and Vietnam in military intelligence—and had a few more careers after he left the military. When he retired from his DuPont Forest volunteer stint, Devendorf was well into his eighties.

Dave Brown came to DuPont Forest in July 2002 as the first professional forest supervisor. His whole career had been spent as a North Carolina forester; his last post was in the North Carolina Forest Service office in Raleigh. By now, the forest was more than ten thousand acres. For a few months, Brown was the only employee. "In general, DuPont Corporation left the forest in good shape," Brown recalls. "The company had a forest management program where they planted and harvested white pine. They also cut down hardwoods."

By the time Brown started working in the forest, most of the trails had already been named. Equestrians created the first trail maps. Some had ridden the land when it was still privately owned. Trail signs were also up, but Brown changed some. Brown worked with the Youthful Offender program and assigned inmates the job of erecting trail signs.

Brown used a combination of volunteers and professional trail builders. DuPont Forest inherited many dead-end trails that were built for timber extraction. These were closed by covering them with brush that had been dragged in to try to obscure the trailhead. Steep trails were rerouted to prevent erosion. They filled in gullies to protect water quality. "What was neat about DuPont Forest is that professional trail builders lived close by. The builders closest to the site always had the lowest bids because they had less distance to travel," Brown says. "Woody Keen's Trail Dynamics got 80 percent of the trail work."

There were so many trails and such a variety of trails—not common in other state forests. The trails may have been wide when they were first built. However, they became single tract trail over time; for example, a six-inch tree might have grown in the middle of what had been a forest road. "The big thing was the cooperation between different trail users," Brown said. "Multi-use trails in forest was new. Most people liked multi-use trails; only a few wanted different trails for different activities." The forest was managed for recreation from the beginning. Water from the falls and lakes was monitored to make sure it was safe. The Wildlife Resource Commission helped to manage the hunting.

"If you want to see the difference, look at Bladen Lakes State Forest in Eastern North Carolina," Brown says. "It was created for timber protection. Most people come to Bladen to hunt. There are few trails, and none are single-track trails." On Wikipedia, Bladen Lakes describes itself as a "working forest, which means it is actively managed and creates its own income. Yearly revenues are generated through timber sales, pine straw sales and cooking of charcoal."

The Forest Grows Up

Dave Brown and his staff quickly realized that they had to develop parking areas. Unlike most parks and forests, visitors cannot drive inside DuPont Forest. People get in by hiking, biking or on horseback, although there are some permits and provisions for visitors with disabilities.

By the time David Brown retired in 2013, he had implemented many changes to the forest. Visitor numbers grew every year. Visitors discovered DuPont Forest, especially after *The Hunger Games* was partially filmed here. *Outside Magazine* named DuPont Forest one of the top five state parks in the country, mentioning "80 miles of world-class mountain biking trails." The magazine got the classification wrong by calling it a park, but the sentiment was accurate.

When Dave Brown retired, he moved to Boonville, North Carolina, west of Winston-Salem where he grew up. He now lives on family land. "I continue to practice forestry on my family property. I have cut and sold forty-eight cords of firewood, mentioning that if cut eighteen inches long and stacked 4 feet high, the stack would be 1,024 feet long." Brown passed on a healthy forest to Jason Guidry, the next forest supervisor.

HIKE: BEWILDERED ON SHEEP MOUNTAIN TRAIL

"Don't confuse the map with the territory!" That's probably my favorite hike saying. But I want to add a second one: "If you think your map is wrong, think again. It's probably you."

When I park on Staton Road at one end of the Sheep Mountain Trail, I'm sure that I'm starting at the Visitor Center end of the trail. Almost as soon as I start hiking, I reach the intersection with Cascade Trail and Pine Trail. I'm confused and blame the map. I walk the whole Sheep Mountain Trail and back.

Sheep Mountain Trail is a double-track trail, really a road. Many mystery holes were dug on the side of the trail, but they're well off the trail and they don't affect hiking or biking. Lots of fresh tire tracks as well. Today, two vehicles are parked on the side of the trail. At the end of the trail, on the right, there's a small pond at the bottom of a sloping creek—another mystery to uncover.

The area off Sheep Mountain Trail was first used to bury waste from the plant site. Then DuPont Corporation created a baseball field on top of the

Opening day for Hubbard Field at the DuPont Brevard plant, 1974. *Courtesy of Chan Hubbard family.*

debris, called Hubbard Field to honor its first employee on the site, Chan Hubbard. The field opened in 1974.

But when the plant closed in 2002, Agfa, the last owner, pulled down all the buildings. DuPont Corporation came back to clean up the area. On Sheep Mountain Trail, it excavated the old film that it had buried under the baseball field. The environmental rule was that the company then needed to restore the field to its natural state before it had made any alterations to the land—that meant before it created the baseball field decades ago.

The remediation team had to reestablish the natural streambed. It placed large flat boulders, creating a little creek where water flows gently. At the bottom, a pool of water contains vegetation scattered about. Several small pines have been planted around the pool. A skimmer, which looks like a child's float, is tied to a rock on the shore. The whole design is meant to slow down water and reinstall its natural flow.

The Forest Grows Up

When I'm on my way back on Sheep Mountain Trail, a large pickup truck ambles along. The driver introduces himself as Mike. "Do you work for the forest service or DuPont?" I ask.

"Neither. I'm on a disability hunt. Today, I'm checking out the trail. Tomorrow I'll hunt." Mike explains that he applied for a disability hunting license earlier in the year. He was one of eight lucky hunters in the whole state of North Carolina chosen by a lottery system. I wish him success on the hunt. He's probably looked forward to this for months.

"So do you hunt from your truck?" I ask.

"No, I have someone helping me." He's not much of a talker and doesn't give details. This is fall and hunters are getting ready.

Most visitors do not appreciate the difference between a forest and park until they learn about hunting. Hunting is allowed in DuPont Forest, but it's very limited: three days a week with a special permit. The hunting area is only on the periphery of the forest, where there are few visitors. In the heavily used sections, safety zones have been established where hunting is forbidden. The Friends of DuPont website states that DuPont Forest is "registered as North Carolina Game Lands, hunting is by lottery only. Deer is typically Friday and Saturday in season; turkey is typically Thursday, Friday and Saturday in season. No Sunday hunting."

After Mike continues on his reconnaissance drive, I meet Lisa, a trail runner. I pull out the DuPont Forest map and tell her my confusion. She set me straight.

"You started much further on Staton Road," she shows me. The map now makes sense. Sheep Mountain Trail is a ragged "C" shape, and I had started at the far end. My well-laid hiking plans for the day are shot, but I still bagged a few new trails.

I need to backtrack on Sheep Mountain Trail and take Pine Tree Trail, a narrow, rocky trail. I don't meet any hunters, just two mountain bikers. The next trail, Twixt Trail, is only 0.4 miles. It's one of those mystery trails—who built this trail and what was its purpose? You can always say for fire access or for logging. Twixt Trail ends at Cascade Lake Road. My car is less than a mile away, so there's no need for me to hitchhike from here. It wasn't a satisfying hike, although I got in a few more miles of my "all the trails in DuPont" project.

STUDYING THE FOREST MANAGEMENT PLAN

A story is told about the beginnings of Yellowstone National Park in 1872. The park's promoters envisioned that Yellowstone would exist at no expense to the government. According to National Park Service history, Nathaniel P. Langford was appointed to the unpaid post of superintendent. He entered the park at least twice during five years in office. Without laws protecting wildlife and other resources and without money to hire rangers, he could not accomplish much. The thinking seemed to be: Why should there be funding for trees and birds? The second superintendent of Yellowstone received a salary and a budget.

When we think about forests, we see trees and wild creatures. Some feel that the best thing is to leave the forest alone. But forests have to be managed, especially when there were prior human activities and now current recreation on the land. Today, there are so many participating interests in DuPont Forest. A white "Share the Trail" sign with a yellow triangle alerts visitors to hikers, bikers and equestrians. But there is so much more: hunting, fishing, endangered species, scientific and educational pursuits and historic preservation. The forest even allows training exercises for military personnel and law enforcement groups. To adapt a Kenny Chesney song, "We can all get along."

To guide forest staff, a sixty-three-page DuPont State Forest Land and Resource Management Plan was published in June 2011, one month before the North Carolina state legislature changed the designation of DuPont Forest to a recreational forest. The document is still relevant until the next management plan is approved. The current plan first describes what is on the property.

DuPont Forest ranges in altitude from 2,240 feet below Hooker Falls at Cascade Lake to 3,620 feet at the top of Stone Mountain. As a comparison, the Pisgah District of Pisgah National Forest in the same general area is 162,000 acres with an altitude ranging from 2,000 feet at the North Carolina Arboretum to 6,410 feet at Richland Balsam. Both forests had a long human history. Wherever people settled, they clear-cut the land for farming and grazing and let it regenerate without replanting trees.

In DuPont Forest, the most abundant natural community is Montane Oak-Hickory. Scarlet oak and white oak are the dominant trees on more than half the land. Widespread American chestnut sprouts are also found here. But pastureland was planted with white pine all at once. Other areas were heavily cut and also replanted with fast-growing trees. Mountain laurel and rhododendrons, both members of the heath family, became the most common understory, probably because of lack of fire. When the American chestnut succumbed to the chestnut blight, heath bushes filled in the gaps. Because of clear-cutting from the 1930s to the 1970s, the trees are of the same age.

Acidic Cove Forests are the next most abundant type, with white pine and yellow poplar dominating. Again, most trees are forty to sixty years old. When the DuPont Corporation owned the land, it created a white pine plantation, which is not the best for forest health. Forests need a balance of early, mid and late forest lands in succession. The conclusion is that more tree diversity in species and ages are needed for a healthier forest.

A very small but interesting area is the Spray Cliff around Triple and High Falls. Bare rocks are constantly sprayed with water. High moisture encourages the spread of mosses and liverworts, a different type of plant community than the rest of the wooded forest.

DuPont Forest participates in the North Carolina Wildlife Resources Commission's Game Land program. The forest wants to encourage good habitat for charismatic game species like deer, turkey, grouse and bear, even though there's no bear hunting at this time. Charismatic animals are large species that visitors hope to see.

Water quality is generally high throughout the Little River and its tributaries. A section of Little River is stocked with trout. Sediment, probably from soil erosion, is the primary threat to water quality. The sediment is carried by wind or water to nearby rivers and lakes. The Environmental Protection Agency states that sediment is the most common pollutant in rivers, streams, lakes and reservoirs:

> *The Little River is classified by NCDEQ as Class C fresh surface water (aquatic propagation and survival, fishing, wildlife, secondary recreation, and agricultural use). In addition, the Little River has a supplemental classification of Class TR (Trout Waters* [intended to protect freshwaters for natural trout propagation and survival of stocked trout]*).*

The Little River has twelve named tributary streams. Four waterfalls lie on Little River. Listed from upstream to downstream, these are Bridal Veil, High Falls, Triple Falls and Hooker Falls. The waterfalls on Grassy Creek, Grassy Creek Falls and Wintergreen are less well-known, perhaps because they require a little more effort to reach.

The water supports cold-water fish above Lake Julia, Lake Imaging and Bridal Veil Falls. Lake Julia, the largest of the lakes at ninety-nine acres, is not good for sports fishing. The other lakes are much smaller. Fawn Lake, only six acres, is a popular swimming spot but also not a great place to fish since it is located near the top of the watershed. Even smaller, Lake Dense, five acres, seems to be the most productive impoundment in DuPont Forest. The lake even attracts snapping turtles.

Lake Imaging is only one acre, but the water temperature is low enough for trout fishing. Because it's the closest lake to parking, it's stocked for special fishing events. Lake Alford, close to Lake Dense, is so small—a half acre—that there's no fishing activity. It is, however, a very picturesque lake, perfect for marriage proposals.

The forest management plan includes a section on demonstration and education. Several trails have a series of large metal signs that describes road and trail construction techniques. These BMPs, or Best Management Practices, are designed to protect water quality. For example, if sediments create the most polluting conditions, then it's important to build and maintain a trail to capture silt and debris before it flows into the river.

This sign, on the Holly Trail, lists the "Keys to Success" and includes in part:

- *Excavate the pit/trap in stable soil—Do not install it within the road fill material.*
- *Use waterbars or broad-based dips to divert water runoff into the sediment trap.*
- *Clean out mud periodically.*

Another sign focuses on daylighting, which involves removing trees to create a corridor wide enough so the road or trail can dry out. These BMPs may sound like common sense, but they must not have been implemented before.

To provide low-impact recreation, trails need to be inspected to assess if they are eroding and causing excess sedimentation. An objective in the report states that all forest trails and roads should be checked annually. Stream crossings on trails and roads are evaluated every year, which should make active visitors very happy.

Forests, whether state or national, don't usually emphasize historical or cultural artifacts. But this land has included so many waves of people that it has many artifacts. Thomas Cemetery and Hooker-Moore Cemeteries are currently maintained by the forest staff and volunteers. A third cemetery off Rock Quarry Road requires a bushwhack through trees and bushes and

The Forest Grows Up

Thomas Cemetery. *Author's collection.*

does not have a sign. But Summit Camps and DuPont Company structures and artifacts must not be considered historic. If the building was not useful, it got taken down.

The management plan also lists a huge number of facilities, from the Visitor Center and restrooms to fishing piers. Some are for public use, such as the picnic shelters and viewing platforms. Others are for staff use, including several ranger houses and equipment sheds. For a small forest, there are a great many structures to maintain.

Where there are land and people, there will be invasive plants, including multiflora rose, Chinese silvergrass and Japanese honeysuckle. This is no different from other public lands in the Southern Appalachians. Some invasive species were invited in because they were decorative, like multiflora rose in front of a cabin. Others just floated in and were spread by birds and people. Sometimes it feels like no amount of pulling and cutting will get rid of all the nonnative plants.

CREATING A RECREATIONAL FOREST

On May 4, 2011, the North Carolina State House of Representatives passed a budget bill that included a provision to move the Division of Forest Resources from the Department of Environment and Natural Resources (DENR) to the Department of Agriculture and Consumer Services (DACS). The Department of Agriculture is primarily focused on farms, meat inspection and livestock marketing, among other responsibilities.

North Carolina Division of Forest Resources belongs within the Department of Agriculture and Consumer Services. Even the name "Resource" was a flag that the division is primarily concerned with timber and mineral extraction. Where would DuPont Forest fit into this new home? This was an important change that raised concerns. A coalition of the major user groups—hikers, bikers, equestrians and hunters—had a series of meetings to talk about the forest.

DuPont Forest could have become a state park and received protection from wholesale logging this way. That was considered and rejected several years ago. The coalition liked the low-key way the current staff manages the forest. Its members just want the forest to continue to be focused mostly on recreation and conservation and protect natural and cultural resources. That required legislation.

North Carolina Representative Chuck McGrady, a member of Friends of DuPont Forest and champion of the forest since the 1990s, and Senator Tom Apodaca drafted a bill that would officially make DuPont Forest a recreational forest, North Carolina's first. Timber would only be cut for forest management—that is, to control fire and pests. If forest managers wanted to harvest trees and sell the lumber, they would have to get permission from the governor and the Council of State.

In the statute Article 74, Acquisition and Control of State Forests and State Recreational Forests, DuPont Forest gets its own subsection entitled "§ 106-887. Management of DuPont State Recreational Forest." Friends of DuPont Forest is mentioned as one of the interested stakeholders. The first paragraph of the statute reads:

> *DuPont State Forest is designated as a State Recreational Forest. The Department shall manage DuPont State Recreational Forest: (i) primarily for natural resource preservation, scenic enjoyment and recreational purposes, including horseback riding, hiking, bicycling, hunting, and fishing; (ii) so as to provide an exemplary model of scientifically sound,*

> *ecologically based natural resource management for the social and economic benefit of the forest's diverse community of users; and (iii) consistent with the grant agreement that designates a portion of the forest as a North Carolina Nature Preserve. In addition, the Department may use the forest for the demonstration of different forest management and resource protection techniques for local landowners, natural resource professionals, students, and other forest visitors.*

Yet trees are still cut, and the resultant lumber can be sold. A timber sale was approved in 2018 in the southern end of the forest around Reasonover Road. The white pines, planted when DuPont Corporation owned the land, were now crowded and damaged from ice. The plan is to replant the area with shortleaf pine, a species that the forest wants to restore.

"These trees get really old and big and start deteriorating," Bruce MacDonald, DuPont Forest's communications director, is quoted in the *Asheville Citizen-Times*. "The idea is to mix species, get more diversity, which improves forest health and improves species composition. More diversity helps wildlife and other aspects of the forest as well." The whole area affected was forty-two acres. The fiscal year annual report from the forest supervisor states that the resulting timber brought in $51,100.

WE CAN ALL GET ALONG

The trails in DuPont Forest are used by many constituents, including hikers, bikers, equestrians, trail runners, baby strollers and dog walkers. Other user groups have found the forest an inviting place for their activities.

Mountain bikers were on the trails from the beginning but have really multiplied now. Biking magazines, mountain biking clubs and word of mouth have spread the reputation of DuPont Forest way beyond the region. *Bike Magazine* uses DuPont Forest trails to test out mountain bikes. It called it one of the best places in America to ride a bike. The magazine described the trails:

> *Some of it swoopy and fast. Some of it rocky and steep. We took some of the best trail bikes on the market up the latter. It's a short loop, but it rises right off the bat and includes some seriously argh-f*cking-argh-style technical climbing before summiting on a nice heap of slickrock that makes*

for a screaming descent full of square edged hits. We did five consecutive laps and called it good, or to be precise, effin' rad.

Other praise for biking in DuPont followed. There's even Pinterest boards on the wonders of biking in DuPont.

Jim Parham, a mountain biker and guidebook writer, explains that what makes DuPont Forest trails so attractive to bikers are the quality of the trails themselves. "Much thought has been put into their design. Turns are banked, steep grades are made easier with multiple and wide switchbacks, and they take you to interesting places," Parham says. The trails in DuPont Forest are easier than nearby Pisgah National Forest, where elevations are much higher. In Pisgah Forests, trails were not initially built with cyclists in mind, and maintenance can use some improvements.

"For instance, if a tree falls across the trail after a storm in Pisgah National Forest," Parham says, "it may stay there for months, where in DuPont Forest the fallen tree is gone by the next day." Many expert riders like DuPont Forest; they just tend to ride faster or farther.

Dave Vance, an accomplished rider from Asheville, rides in both DuPont Forest and Pisgah Forest. "You can ride faster and longer in DuPont Forest. It might take three hours in Pisgah for thirteen miles, let's say Turkey Pen to Mullinax Trail. In the same three hours, I can ride twenty-five miles in DuPont Forest."

Vance says that he can ride any trail in DuPont Forest without getting off the bike. Not so in Pisgah, where he might be pushing his bike uphill on some trails. "Some people aren't having any fun in Pisgah. It's too steep, more technical. With rocks, roots, that have consequences if you fall."

Vance also takes his two children, now young teens, riding in DuPont Forest. The three ride together; they also belong to Pisgah Rage, part of National Interscholastic Cycling Association for students from sixth grade to twelfth grade, where they ride with other family groups in organized activities from pleasure rides to races.

Sara Landry, executive director of Friends of DuPont Forest, considers herself a moderate cyclist. She can get a good workout and challenge herself. "There are good options for fun downhills that I can do without dying," she laughs. She finds Pisgah National Forest too steep and technical with lots of drops, rocks, roots and other things she cannot navigate. She describes the trails in DuPont Forest as "flowy." "I can do a group ride with super experienced riders and beginners and we all can go home happy," she adds. Everyone agrees that the most important thing is to be able to ride again the next day.

The Forest Grows Up

Kids' bike rally at Guion Farm Access Area. *Author's collection.*

It's not common to meet someone on horseback in DuPont Forest, but it's always a pleasure. On the trail, horses walk slowly with a majestic manner. Equestrians have done a great deal to shape DuPont Forest trails.

Gwen Hill rode her horse in the forest when the land was still owned by DuPont Corporation. She came on the property as a guest of an employee. Hill worked at Eckerd Wilderness Camp, a year-round facility for children ages ten to seventeen who were troubled or difficult to manage. The camp bordered the DuPont property and was allowed to use its land. Hill was able to organize fundraising events for equestrians to help the camp.

There were ATV and equestrian clubs for employees. Hill recalls that DuPont Corporation stopped the ATV club because the company felt that ATVs were ruining the trails. "DuPont was very active in the community. Everyone loved them," Hill says.

Hill and other equestrians knew the trails well. When the forest was created, she took forest administrators to show them the property. Ed Goforth, the assistant regional forester, and Hill created the first trail maps. "In those days, I knew the trails," Hill says. "I had created a little hand-drawn map."

Horse people used funny names to refer to the trails. "When we found what is now called Wintergreen Falls," Hill says, "it was because Sara Cathey and I were trying to find her coon dog which had no hair on its tail. So we called the waterfall 'Possum Tail Falls.' The dog had chased a deer and was standing at the falls. Our volunteer group also called the creek crossing at Lake Julia dam 'Little Wyoming' because it made us think of water crossings out west." The huge pile of rocks and debris on Joanna Road, probably caused by a dynamite explosion, was dubbed "Damnation Ridge."

Forest service rangers renamed the trails, using designations from nature like Pine Tree Trail and Twin Oaks. They also recalled those who lived here before it was a forest and honored Ben Cart, owner of Summit Camps; Micajah Thomas, one of the first settlers; and Isaac Heath, who is buried at the Hooker-Moore Cemetery. The two major roads that bisect the forest vertically, Buck Forest and Conservation Roads, might have been on the ground before DuPont Corporation came along.

Hill recalls that horse people were the first forest volunteers. "But now I feel it's too dangerous for horses." Bikers don't look ahead of them and can be right on top of a horse. She had suggested that different user groups come on different days. "But the suggestion was never taken up."

Pisgah Trailblazers, the equestrian group, made the first trail signs. It started by blazing trees. Later, it had laminated wood signs. On other trails, paper signs were covered in a plastic bag and tacked on trees.

Today, Pisgah Trailblazers do trail work, repair fences, pick up litter, have monthly work weekend campouts and do other projects to keep trails open for all user groups. When members work in DuPont Forest, they can stay at the horse barn. Jackie West, a current Trailblazer, recalls that "we as a group have worked on many trails, under the supervision of David Brown, who was the head forest ranger out there for many years. The major work such as redirecting or building trails is done by machines, of course, but we've built fences, improved trails, cut trees, built mounting blocks, painted—you name it."

Jackie West rides just about every week. "I know the trails inside and out, backwards and forwards," she says. "I also ride at Biltmore, Pisgah, Mills River, South Mountains, but I enjoy the trails at DuPont over the others. The trails drain nicely, and I feel safe here, even riding alone (which I usually do). There are always bikers, hikers and other equestrians around in the event of a need."

There's an accepted hierarchy regarding who yields to whom. Signs are posted at almost every major trail intersection. Hikers yield to horse riders. Bikers yield to everyone. In reality, when mountain bikers swoop down a steep trail at who knows how many miles an hour, they are not going to

Above: The horse barn, built for Summit Camps, is still in use. *Author's collection.*

Right: "Share the Trail" sign on DuPont Forest trails. *Author's collection.*

stop dead for hikers. Instead, hikers coming up the trail move to the side and wait for them to pass.

The different user groups tend to self-regulate. Traditionally, they congregated in different parts of the forest. Corn Mill Shoals trailhead attracts predominately bikers. Lake Imaging and Guion Farm Access Areas sees lot of horse use. And most hikers show up at the main entrance at High Falls trailhead. That formula is changing as the forest becomes well known.

But the type of user grows along with the number of visitors. Twice a year, the Pack Llama Trial Association congregates in DuPont Forest to train and certify llamas. During this trial, newbie llamas will go on a three-mile hike carrying panniers that weigh 10 percent of their own body weight. If they pass, the llamas will become certified as Basic Pack Llamas. The advanced llamas will walk five miles with up to a thousand feet of elevation gain while carrying 15 percent of their body weight. The Pack Trials take place on Easter and Thanksgiving. The organization favors these periods with the best weather for llamas to pack in, since the holiday seasons tends to have moderate weather.

SPEAKING WITH FOREST SUPERVISOR JASON GUIDRY

When Jason Guidry became the second forest supervisor at DuPont Forest in 2013, the forest attracted fewer than 400,000 visitors. Now it's more than 860,000 and destined to hit a million soon.

Guidry replaced the retiring Dave Brown, the first forest supervisor, who left a terrific legacy. Guidry is a native of Clay County in the far western part of North Carolina. Armed with a degree in biology from University of North Carolina–Chapel Hill and an MS in forestry at NC State, he has worked in wetland restoration and soil conservation. Before coming to DuPont Forest, he was a county forester in Clay County. Six years later, he is still excited about working with stakeholders: hikers, bikers, equestrians—and there are plenty of those.

"The 2011 Management Plan is still relevant, but it need updating," Guidry says. "It doesn't have a recreational component. We need to add that."

Guidry sees DuPont as a hybrid of park and forests. "Park" seems to be synonymous with public lands. "We stress the uniqueness of DuPont Forest." In general, forests have fewer rules than parks. The average state forest doesn't

The Forest Grows Up

Forest Supervisor Jason Guidry talks to visitors. *Courtesy of the North Carolina Forest Service.*

expect a lot of visitors. DuPont Forest has three law enforcement rangers on staff. Unlike North Carolina State Park rangers, other forest rangers, in general, do not carry guns and are not responsible for law enforcement. "In the past, I wanted everyone to know it's a forest. Now I'm ambivalent."

With almost one hundred miles of trail now, "we don't look at all trails yearly. We look for erosion. We also have eyes and ears to the ground. We'll ask if this trail is necessary. What does the trail system need? We need to relook at trails that are unsustainable. Every trail is someone's favorite," Guidry says.

He and his wife live on the DuPont Forest property with their two school-age children. The children grasp how unique their environment is. They'll appreciate it more later. When friends visit, the Guidry children are proud of where they live, even though they have a long ride to the Brevard schools. The school bus picks them up just outside the forest. "There are three rangers living here. We're available for quick searches and 911 calls. We maintain a presence in the forest, but how do you get away from work?" Guidry asks. The other sixteen full-time employees live off site.

"We're dealing with a lot of visitors. In 2011, who could have predicted the popularity of *The Hunger Games*? An international sensation."

The North Carolina Forest Service and Friends of DuPont Forest are working on an MOU (Memorandum of Understanding). "The Friends need to find projects that members are excited about and are willing to fund," Guidry says.

He summarizes his future challenges as looking at infrastructure, a solid plan for recreation management and a budget. "We need to make the funding sustainable." Guidry had proposed an entrance fee a few years ago. It is now being taken up by the North Carolina legislature. "We don't want to price people out of the experience."

But like everyone who loves the forest, Guidry is frustrated by the trash and other vandalism that careless visitors leave behind. Before the 2019 Friends of DuPont Forest annual meeting, he took a hike from the Visitor Center to High Falls and Triple Falls, the most popular part of the forest. Carrying a camera and trash bags, he brought back more than forty pounds of garbage. His photos showed etching of initials on trees and visitor-created social trails branching off official trails.

"This is only a mile and a half of trail," Guidry says. "This is happening almost everywhere." While he did not come to the meeting looking for solutions, he wanted to reach more people with the Leave No Trace ethic.

Land conservancies are proposing adding more land to DuPont Forest. "It's not an open door. It means more area to patrol and to maintain," Guidry says. The newest acquisitions are the Picklesimer property and the Continental Divide tract. Natural communities and recreational opportunities have to be evaluated. It will take at least two years to study these new lands. The land has to be surveyed by the North Carolina Natural Heritage Program.

"DuPont Corporation left us amazing things," Guidry says. "If they hadn't owned it, it would have been subdivided into five hundred properties. Look at the rest of the land."

HIKE: WALKING JOANNA ROAD FROM BOTH DIRECTIONS

Sometimes driving to the trailhead is the most difficult part of the hike. In my attempt to walk every trail in DuPont Forest, I thought it was high time to go past the popular trailheads. Joanna Road at 4.2 miles may be the longest continuous trail in the forest; on the *National Geographic* map, it is labeled "difficult."

The Forest Grows Up

The trail bisects the forest west–east. The western end is very easy to reach from Conservation Road, but the eastern access starts from Pinnacle Mountain Road. I had been warned that Pinnacle Mountain Road was rutted and full of large potholes.

"I wouldn't take my car up there unless it had a lot of clearance," people said. And I listened. I leaned on Tom Lucha and his truck again; he was eager to explore the area as well. Maybe he didn't really want to explore it, but I sweet-talked him into it. What is the good of a truck if you don't use it on roads that shouldn't be driven by passenger cars? Lucha brought a neighbor. I asked Sharon, a hiking friend, if she was interested in a different type of hike and maybe an adventure.

Today, we meet at the Fawn Lake Access Area, where we all leave our cars and pile into Lucha's truck. The plan was to hike together for a while. Then the men would drive back to Hendersonville while Sharon and I would hike down to Fawn Lake, using various trails. DuPont Forest has so many trails and so many short segments with quick turns that I always create a spreadsheet of our plans. Sharon and I would walk 12.7 miles, not a great challenge in the forest.

From the Fawn Lake parking area, we drive on Reasonover Road, a paved road lined with houses, most set back and out of sight. As soon as we turn on Pinnacle Mountain Road, I see and feel that it's as challenging as advertised. Potholes are filled with water. They act as speed bumps on sections of the road that don't need bumps. Large stretches are filled with mud and cracked concrete. The road to our trailhead is only about four miles, but Lucha takes it slowly.

An old faded yellow post with "Joanna Rd." stenciled in tells us we've arrived at the trailhead. We start the hike together. You can see that it was a road at some point. We quickly turn on Grassy Meadow Trail. "You go on," Lucha says to Sharon and me. "You're much faster." We pass a large meadow filled with bushes and a few autumn flowers—it's late July. A narrow path goes around the meadow, and a much clearer trail takes us right and past the meadow. There's no sign, but we feel that the trail on the right is the obvious one.

How many hiking brains does it take to get confused in DuPont Forest? And how did it happen? DuPont State Recreational Forest is signposted well. Every intersection is marked by large, accurate trail signs. But still we were bewildered. Sharon and I reach a campground with several trails shooting off in different directions. That's a bad sign because DuPont Forest doesn't have campgrounds on its property. Maybe it's a campground left over from the DuPont Company days, when employees could camp on the property. When I start making rationalizations, I know that I'm clutching at straws.

Not a trail sign in sight. We choose a trail to the left and climb. Could we still be on Grassy Meadow Trail? The trail takes us up to a knoll and stops. We retrace our steps back to the campsite. This is where we meet our companions again. The two men had taken another trail off the campground and reached a lake. They were on private property—now we all are. Then we remember the narrow, overgrown trail that went left around Grassy Meadows that we ignored. We turn back and take that trail, where there's a clear forest trail sign.

We're back on track, but by now it's almost noon. Sharon and I scuttle our plans to walk back to Fawn Lake. We continue on Joanna Road and catch Briery Fork and Twin Oaks Trails but return with the guys on Pinnacle Mountain Road.

A fact about DuPont Forest is reinforced. Here, every intersection is marked. If it's not signposted, it's not a real intersection. Studying the DuPont Forest map and doing a few internet searches, I think the lake was Lake Louellen, part of St. Francis by the Lake Chapel. But I still have miles of Joanna Road to explore.

To hike the rest of Joanna Road, I need to start from Conservation Road to walk where I left off the last time. It's only a few weeks later, but now an early autumn feeling has set in. Tall scarlet cardinal flowers in late summer can't be missed. *Fecundity*—that's the word for today's hike. All around, it's green, wet, moist and lush. I'm the first person on the trail this morning, and I break up elaborate spider webs with my pole and sometimes my face. Mother and daughter white mushrooms dot the trail.

I'm alone because I can't see asking someone else to hike a simple there-and-back trail. When I walk by myself, my to-do list runs through my head. I try to identify flowers to slow down my monkey mind. The vegetation is a mixture of native and nonnative invasive species like morning glory vines.

Chestnut Oak Road is an uphill graveled road that links two major roads, Joanna Road and Buck Forest Road. Originally, this was a working area, not made for recreation. A park might have named it Chestnut Road for the chestnut trees, but these were sensible owners—they knew that chestnut trees were long gone. Back on Joanna Road, I come up on a large rock pile, probably an old stone quarry. Beautiful stone steps were built, but they seem to be going no place, just for show.

On Table Rock Trail, I pick up trash, a sure sign that I've bonded with the forest. Past the three popular waterfalls, there usually is a little garbage. But here on this obscure trail, I find a beer can and plastic water bottle. Why is this good trail out here? I was expecting a view at the top, but it's a forested knoll. Maybe it's better in winter when the leaves are down. A steep trail continues past the top. I go down about halfway as the trail gets narrower and then turn around. Maybe this was a good hunting spot when the DuPont Corporation owned the land or even before that.

I retrace my steps and make a stop at Grassy Creek Falls. The water is running high, taking full advantage of the steady rain we've had for the last few days. This waterfall doesn't make a good picture, since you can only photograph it from the middle, not at the bottom. After a long-abandoned barbecue pit, the trail is blocked with a "Do Not Enter" sign.

I sit on rocks by Hilltop Trail and eat lunch. By noon, mountain bikers and hikers have come out. A family reaches Grassy Creek Trail, where a sign asks bikers to dismount and walk the few hundred yards to the falls. They hesitate, each waiting for the other to decide. This is the time where problems are bound to occur. Sure enough, the ten-year-old boy drops his bike on his foot.

"Would you like a Band-Aid?" I offer.

"No. He's all right," his father says. But the boy is not all right; he complains that his foot is still hurting. Some walk their bikes to the falls. The women leave their bikes, taking their phones, and walk. That's the smarter way to get to Grassy Creek Falls.

BLOCKBUSTERS IN THE FOREST

DuPont Forest is a natural setting for movies. Characters can be shown deep in the forest surrounded by trees while they make use of mountain biking trails and wide roads. In other scenes, waterfalls may be the star feature. The characters can go places that are off-limits to visitors and show what lies above or behind the waterfalls. Some movies have gone on to international fame and lasting power. Others have led a quiet death at the box office or have never been shown in the movie theaters. But DuPont Forest shines, no matter the film's fate.

Until *The Last of the Mohicans* was screened in the movie theaters in 1992, most people had never seen the DuPont waterfalls. While the company owned the land, outsiders could come in with the proper permissions. However, one could not casually put on hiking boots and walk to a waterfall. The movie was partly filmed in DuPont Forest, with scenes at Triple, Hooker and Bridal Veil Falls. The story, set in Upstate New York in 1757, is from the James Fenimore Cooper classic. It tells the tale of the English and French armies who are battling for control of the North American colonies; this war is known as the French and Indian War. A young, athletic Daniel Day-Lewis plays a White man raised by Mohicans, and beautiful Madeleine Stowe is the daughter of an English officer.

War strategy, mayhem and massacre dominate the film, but a love story inevitably develops between the two leads. The English group always seem to be moving to get away first from the French and then from Indian warriors allied with the French. First, they go up Triple Falls, climbing to the top part of the waterfall. The Madeline Stowe character is able to negotiate the rock face in her long dress and shoes that the audience never sees. Later, canoes plunge into Hooker Falls, but somehow they all survive. Toward the end of the movie, a smaller group finds Bridal Veil Falls and hides behind in caves. There are no caves in Bridal Veil Falls—that was a movie set.

The Last of the Mohicans was filmed in other locations around Western North Carolina as well. Soon after the group feels safe enough to leave the fictional caves, they're walking on a ledge. A new waterfall appears, but that's in Chimney Rock State Park, almost sixty miles away by modern roads. Somehow, the movie has endured and is not forgotten. What makes it still relevant almost thirty years later?

Max, shot in DuPont Forest, also makes use of the waterfalls. It's a sweet story of a family torn apart when their older son, Kyle, is killed in Afghanistan. Kyle handled Max, a majestic dog trained to alert its owner to dangerous combat situations. But Kyle is gone, and his younger brother, Justin, unravels the secret behind his death.

In the movie, Justin and his friends spend a lot of time mountain biking in the forest. They're tearing through the trails and jumping over huge chasms with help from movie magic. They cross Hooker Falls with their bikes to get away from the bad guys and magically end up at the rock quarry, miles away. In one scene, Justin and Max are hurt but manage to hitch a ride on Staton Road on their first try. A kind old lady races them to the veterinarian in Brevard. Now that's movie magic!

But how and where do the movie companies set up for these complex filming operations? Chet Meinzer, the DuPont property manager, explains that base camp was always in a huge empty parking area, now located on the closed donut hole. The movie people set up their trailers here. Wide roads, still closed to the public, are available to transport people and equipment to various locations.

The North Carolina Forest Service may not be able to charge the film company that uses the forest, but it does charge for its staff time. The DuPont Forest staff works with the movie director to ensure that they don't hurt the resources and, in turn, work safely. But Meinzer, who allows the movie companies to set up their base camp on current DuPont Corporation property, has no such restrictions; he charges them and donates the proceeds to various local nonprofit organizations.

Movie magic has certainly helped make *The Hunger Games* the exciting film that it is. Almost all of the movie scenes were filmed in North Carolina in 2011. This film was the most famous of the movies shot in DuPont Forest. The forest was at its best and most lush in late spring and summer. Katniss, the heroine, must survive in the DuPont wilderness.

Airstrip Trail was used via the magic of CGI to create the views from the train windows. A wide-angle lens was affixed on a helicopter that flew over the airstrip, filming the forest on either side. A train was superimposed on the airstrip to give the impressions that Katniss and her love interest, Peeta, are traveling through District 12 to the Capitol.

Here, the exploding trees around Katniss were propane-powered trees made out of pipe. At some point, Katniss runs across Triple Falls; it's not a good idea to run across a waterfall. Bruce MacDonald, communications director for the forest, is quoted as saying, "What people don't know is that she had a wire holding her from above, and boards to run on below. It is impossible to run across the top of a waterfall. You will die." Climbing a waterfall is never a good idea. Katniss discovers Peeta disguised as a rock next to the waterfall.

After the movie came out, Hunger Games Unofficial Tours sprang up. Fans could travel to many of the film locations, including walking to Triple Falls. Some of the advertised tours include film locations, tour guides, hands-on activities (such as archery lessons and Archery Tag), photo opportunities and bonding with other fans.

Many other movies and commercials have been filmed in DuPont Forest, but it's *The Hunger Games* that drew the most new visitors. And once they learned what was in the forest, they kept coming back.

VISITING THE DONUT HOLE

While visitor numbers increase in the forest, DuPont Corporation continues to clean up what is known as the donut hole, a 476-acre plot in the middle of the forest. This was where Agfa, the last owner, operated the plant before it closed in 2002.

An ecological assessment of the donut hole was done in 2011 by URS Corporation, an international engineering firm. It performed a desktop review using online data and came to the site twice. It visited in early May to see the "emergence of ephemeral vegetation" and "breeding bird activities." Its second visit was in August of the same year to appraise the land when it was fully covered with vegetation.

It found the Lake DERA marsh a highlight of the site. The marsh was nationally rated as a Significant Natural Heritage Area. The report states that this habitat was probably a result of actually building Lake DERA. The wetland has not been disturbed for many years, encouraging a diversity of vegetation. It supports a large community of swamp pink, a threatened species. Swamp pink is only found in freshwater wetlands along streams. Green salamanders, the only salamander listed as endangered, have been found in several sites in the donut hole.

At the end of 2016, DuPont Corporation donated the donut hole, the last piece of land, to the forest. Supporters of the forest were ecstatic. But the cleanup continues. During the forty-four years that the plant operated, it created many Solid Waste Management Sites (SWMS). Some SWMS were filled with office waste, while others held construction debris or defective plastic. According to the 2016 Remedial Action Plans, "DuPont reacquired the divested property in 2006 to maximize control of future potential environmental response actions." While the donut hole is now officially part of the forest, it is not ready for public access. The closed DuPont plant is not a Superfund site. The company, long gone, is back cleaning the site and will continue to clean it up until EPA, the North Carolina Department of Environmental Quality and probably several other agencies says it's done.

I've been trying to get on the closed DuPont property for more than a year now. Finally, I received an invitation to visit the donut hole from Chet Meinzer, the DuPont Corporation property manager of the closed site.

I meet Meinzer at the locked gate hidden in plain sight. He's the "last man standing" who still works for a DuPont-related company to oversee the cleanup. In his sixties, he's a handsome man who exudes health and vitality. He takes me to the DuPont Manufacturing Visitor Center, a 1970s building

The Forest Grows Up

Chet Meinzer manages the environmental cleanup of the DuPont Corporation property. *Author's collection.*

originally constructed to host DuPont clients. This structure is unrelated to the public DuPont Forest Visitor Center. The building is located at the edge of Lake DERA, where employees and their families and guests used to spend their leisure time.

Meinzer started with the DuPont Corporation in 1973 in Parlin, New Jersey, after getting a mechanical engineering degree from Fairleigh Dickinson University. He was project manager for various construction work. In 1989, Meinzer moved to the Brevard plant to build what turned out to be the last structure on the site, a film coating facility erected in 1993. When Agfa, the last owner, closed the plant in 2002, Meinzer stayed on to manage the cleanup.

The property is now completely razed except for this Visitor Center, also used by the North Carolina Forest Service. The large conference room has a stone fireplace, wooden beams and floor-to-ceiling windows. In the back are several small offices. The coat racks hold a large assortment of North Carolina Forest Service beige shirts, ready for whatever size is needed at the moment.

A Customer Tech Center sat close to the road. Customers came here if they had any problems with their film. In general, DuPont Corporation did not make finished products or deal with the end user. The X-ray film business in Brevard was an exception.

Meinzer is in charge of regulatory compliance. Agfa had the responsibility of taking down the buildings, which it completed in 2006. D.H. Griffin Wrecking Company razed the buildings; it was the lead demolition consultant at Ground Zero following the 9/11 terrorist attack in 2001. Meinzer worked with a checklist to ensure that any hazardous material was removed before Griffin demolished the buildings. The checklist is not a two-page sheet attached to a clipboard. Meinzer shows me huge three-ring binders with signoffs on the most minute details. A compliance verification audit was done building by building. Anything that could be reused or recycled was removed.

After the property was flattened, Agfa turned over the site back to DuPont Corporation for underground cleanup. In one area, it pulled out more than 36 million pounds of polyethylene terephthalate (PET), a byproduct of the

Compliance Verification Audit pre-demolition checklist. *Author's collection.*

film manufacturing process. PET is the most common thermoplastic polymer resin of the polyester family, used in fibers for clothing and containers for liquids and foods. Fleece jackets are made from PET, a convenient alternative to wool. About ten years ago, this film byproduct was shipped to Asia, where it could be reused and repurposed.

"We went through everything and took out all the recyclable and recapped the rest," Meinzer says. Recapping means to put soil above the landfill and then seed the area. Manufacturing plant cleanup comes with its own vocabulary.

On the site tour, Meinzer points out where the various film manufacturing buildings used to be. I try to look around and take notes. I jump in and out of his large van for photographs. The property is completely empty except for the Visitor Center building. You can see the remains of large parking lots. It feels like a ghost town with its overgrown grass. He points out the parking lot used for *The Hunger Games* movie crew.

At its height, more than 1,500 employees worked here at DuPont Corporation in three shifts. It was very important to keep the plants running continuously 24/7. "You shut down the polymerization plant for a couple of hours, you're out for a month" says Meinzer. "The stuff would solidify." Employees all parked in the same large concrete lot and had to walk to their individual buildings. There had to be street lighting for the night shift.

"Oh yes," Meinzer says. "It was lit like New York City." The site was like a city. DuPont had a medical infirmary with two doctors and four nurses. It had its own fire trucks and plows and, at times, helped out Transylvania County with cleaning icy roads. The plant had its own potable water; it treated the water from the Little River.

DuPont Corporation built two roads leading to the plant area. The road straight ahead leads to the plant. The road to the right was the construction entrance. Several new buildings went up, while the rest of the plant was operating at full tilt. If construction workers called a strike, only the construction entrance would be affected. As it was, there was never a strike by unionized construction workers. Meinzer recalls a demonstration by Tennessee Greenpeace protesters against Freon in the early 1990s, part of a national movement.

I was hoping to see a settling pond, but all have already been drained and cleaned. The polishing pond, the last treatment stage before the wastewater can eventually be discharged into natural bodies of water, is surrounded by trees. Now the land is a mixture of grasses, trees, cracked parking areas and a few roads. Vegetation is rising from cracks in the concrete where the buildings stood. Undisturbed areas like this encourage wildlife. A wide trail to the left leads to the High Falls/Buck Forest Road area, now marked with a large "Keep Out" sign from the North Carolina Forest Service.

A Property Control Plan is being established to spell out how to take care of the donut hole. About 100 acres of the 476-acre site will be inside a fence line to protect visitors, although Chet Meinzer thinks it will probably be a stone barrier, which looks more natural. Within the boundaries, there should not be any camping or digging. The State of North Carolina will have to inspect the site yearly to ensure that no erosion has taken place on top of the landfill. Jamie Van Buskirk and his staff are working with the North Carolina Forest Service to ensure they have the technical know-how to carry on the minor long-term obligations that will remain after DuPont Corporation finishes the last large-scale remedial actions.

When you ask Forest Supervisor Jason Guidry when the donut hole will be incorporated and visitors will be able to use it, he says, "In a few years.… It will take that long partly because of safety concerns and partly to allow the forest service to plan for the recreational uses compatible with natural resource protection."

HOLMES EDUCATIONAL STATE FOREST: DUPONT FOREST'S SMALLER FRIEND

DuPont Forest keeps getting bigger and better known. Each year, the forest amasses more land and more visitors. But usually it's the parking areas and Visitor Center that are crowded, not the trail. Outside of the three-waterfall area, if you walk a mile from your car, you'll see few people.

If visitors want to get away from the supposed crowds of the DuPont Forest waterfall area, they should visit Holmes Educational State Forest. Holmes is close to DuPont Forest, almost touching across Old CCC Road and administered by the same forest management. I wanted to see this small 235-acre forest and walk its five miles of trail. Susan Fay is the forest supervisor with two education rangers on her staff and lots of volunteers to help them with special projects on the ground.

The forest has its roots in the Civilian Conservation Corps (CCC) of the 1930s. The state bought the property, which had been pastureland, and turned it into a tree nursery. Here it grew white pines and yellow poplar. The CCC boys built the office Fay and I are standing in now and built the supervisor's house where she lives. Her house peeks out of the trees up on a small hill. In this nursery, they attempted to grow Fraser firs in the 1950s for the Christmas trees market, but the valley is just too low in altitude. Fraser firs, in their natural state, are usually seen up on Mount Mitchell and Clingmans Dome, both over well over six thousand feet. The Fraser tree operation was moved to the Linville area, where it's still functioning successfully.

The forest was named for John Simcox Holmes, who became North Carolina's first forester in 1909. It officially became a state forest in 1977, with a niece of the first forester cutting the ribbon. At its start, Holmes State Forest had a picnic area and a campsite. Beyond managing the land, the forest was meant to educate local landowners in sound forestry principles. In the 1980s, it became an educational forest, focusing on environmental education.

"We now have seven educational forests in the state," Fay says as she rattles them off. "Unlike recreational forests like DuPont, there are no horses or bikes here, and we're too small for hunting. It's just walking." Now the educational program focusses on environmental education for schoolchildren. Their biggest pool of visitors are second and third graders and the local community. "We focus on fire, weather, forest environment and water." Last year, 36,800 people visited the forest, compared with almost 900,000 visitors in DuPont Forest.

The area around the parking lot has most of the attractions on the ground. There are "talking trees" throughout a cove forest. If you push a button on an information station, the tree will tell you a little about itself. The biggest hit with children must be the yellow Huey helicopter, one of the most recognizable symbols of the Vietnam War. Now they're used for fire suppression because of their quick starts, tight landings and capability to hover over ridgetops. The helicopters used by the North Carolina Forest Service, including the one on the ground here, were used in the war.

The Demonstration Trail, a three-mile trail, starts with a sign that warns hikers that the trail will take at least two hours. The trail zigzags up the hill lined with rhododendrons and Christmas ferns. A hand-drawn sign with cartoonish figures states that the trail was built by the CCC. At the top, from a wooden observation platform, a few houses and trailers are visible. With only 235 acres, you're bound to see outside the boundaries of the forest.

At the top, the trail makes a long loop. White pines and more white pines of every size. A small nameless pond with a wood duck nesting box in the water looks almost like it was placed here just for visitors. Susan Fay speculates that the pond was probably built for irrigation. There's no graffiti

A Huey helicopter can be seen at Holmes Educational State Forest. *Author's collection.*

A trail sign on the Demonstration Trail at Holmes Educational State Forest. *Author's collection.*

and no garbage on the trail. I would like to think that hikers were especially neat and considerate here, but it probably means that few people come up this trail. Fay concurs: "Very few people go up on the Demonstration Trail. The parking lot can be packed down below, and there's no one on the mountain." She is surprised that the forest has no sign of human remains. She has never found arrowheads or old bottles. "They didn't have trash pickup in the 1930s."

Holmes Forest is all about educating the public on natural resources, biodiversity and the forest environment. But the forest is not free from invasive plants. They have their share of Chinese silvergrass, multiflora rose and ornamental bittersweet. "It would be easier if we sprayed to get rid of invasives, but we don't. Volunteers come out and pull the roses by hand," Fay says.

Susan Fay is in her seventeenth year as a forester. She says that she started her career late in life. She studied natural resources at NC State. Her first job was as an assistant county ranger in Wake Forest close to the North Carolina Capitol. "I was on call all the time," Fay says, "which didn't work well with being a mom." In 2004, she went back to the North Carolina Forest Service as an educational ranger. She moved to Holmes Forest in 2012. "I live on site. It seems like I never leave this place, but it's free rent." Sometimes she misses the city life and city lights. "I'm used to the big cities in the Triangle."

"I think that the cliffs saved the land and the biodiversity," Fay says. "I am amazed how nature will come back and how strongly it will come back."

PART VII
The Future of DuPont Forest

PAY TO PLAY IN THE FOREST?

DuPont State Recreational Forest is getting very popular. With hiking, biking, horse riders and just plain nature lovers, it's predicted that there will be more than a million visitors again in 2020. So it is inevitable that people responsible for the forest are thinking of charging an entrance fee for the forest.

The first proposal came in 2016 when visitation shot up to a million people for a year. Higher fees would be charged for higher-use areas, namely Hooker Falls and High Falls. At the time, those two waterfalls and Triple Falls on the way attracted 75 percent of visitors. The plan called for a daily fee of eight dollars per vehicle Monday through Thursday and twelve dollars on weekends and holidays. Annual passes would be available—thirty dollars for North Carolina residents and seventy dollars for out-of-state visitors. The forest gets many South Carolinians who would probably buy an out-of-state pass. Greenville is less than forty miles from the forest. In total, half the visitors are from out of state.

The fees never went into effect. The North Carolina General Assembly felt that the plan needed more evaluation. Instead, DuPont Forest received nine more staff positions. By the end of 2016, the budget of $3.6 million also included money for a new bathroom, parking lot improvements and new staffing. The bathroom at Hooker Falls became a reality in 2019; Friends of DuPont Forest contributed $50,000 for this amenity. There was a grand opening with an official ribbon cutting and celebration.

By 2019, the fee issue had been brought up again, this time by the state legislature. State Senator Chuck Edwards, a Republican from Hendersonville, filed a bill (SB390) that would direct a commission to study whether and how to charge entrance fees for the forest. SB390 passed the senate unanimously and went to the North Carolina House of Representatives. It received a favorable report in the House State and Local Government Committee and was referred to the House Rules Committee. The bill cleared all the hurdles, and North Carolina governor Roy Cooper signed SB390 into law.

The law states in part that the commission should set fees to favor North Carolinians and require out-of-staters to pay more. This seems fair, as the forest is funded by North Carolina taxpayers. It also asks the committee to look at how other states implement these fees. And here's the problem: DuPont Forest may feel like a state park, but it is a forest. In general, forests do not expect a lot of visitors. Forests protect natural resources, but they also cut timber and allow hunting. Most state forests in North Carolina don't have many trails or bikers.

Several North Carolina state parks charge an entrance fee in the summer months, especially if the main attraction is swimming or boating. The entrance to Chimney Rock State Park is seventeen dollars; Grandfather Mountain charges twenty-two dollars for a day pass. Both parks have attractions and amenities that made them popular when they were private concerns. Grandfather Mountain has the swinging bridge; Chimney Rock has a maze of steps along with an elevator to go up to the rock. These features are expensive to maintain.

South Carolina has charged an entrance fee for its state parks for a long time. For the best deal, one can buy an "All Park Passport" for $99, which provides unlimited entry to all South Carolina state parks for everyone in the pass holder's vehicle. Seniors pay half price. The day fee for Jones Gap State Park in Upstate South Carolina is $6.00 ($3.75 for seniors) per person.

It's not clear how the DuPont Forest fee will be implemented. Will there be gates and rangers checking passes? There are five access areas at DuPont Forest. Do they put gates on all five? Just the Visitor Center lot, since that's the most crowded? A lot to think about. It will be a while before visitors will have to pay to play in DuPont Forest.

KIWI GELATO IN BREVARD

Brevard is home to many people and businesses that have only known DuPont as a state forest. They and their families were not born here, nor were they connected to the DuPont plant. They've come to Brevard to start a business or to leave the more crowded areas they've lived in. The future of the forest belongs to those who've come to love DuPont Forest for its beauty and recreational opportunities.

Richard Coadwell is Kiwi Gelato, and Kiwi Gelato would not exist without Richard Coadwell. A sign in his shop says that a kiwi can be the bird, the fruit or the shop owner. Although he may not be behind the counter all the time, he calls himself the only "full-blooded New Zealander" in the store. The small shop on East Main Street in downtown Brevard is part of a larger movement of newcomers who are not connected with its industrial past.

I get to the store at 9:00 a.m. and find Coadwell already in the back working on his laptop. He greets me and offers me a coffee, although his store is still closed. I immediately lapse into New Zealand talk and ask him for a "flat white done right."

An older man, probably retired, comes by but sees that Coadwell is busy and leaves. "Who's he?" I ask. "Oh, he's my adopted uncle. He's retired and comes by here, and we talk about stuff in the morning, the community, nothing in particular."

Coadwell was born in Christchurch, New Zealand, in a hospital that no longer exists. After graduating from the University of Canterbury in marketing and sales, he worked in sales and became the marketing manager of a large medical supply company.

The country is a favorite destination for adventurous people from the Northern Hemisphere. He met Heather, an American who was working in New Zealand for a few years. They married with the understanding that they would go back to the United States, specifically to settle in Brevard, where her sister lived.

Coadwell had been in the United States around 1990 on a driving tour with a friend. After meeting Heather, he stopped in Brevard in 2005 and spent a few days here. "It looked like a fun place. Lots of people of the same age, playing ultimate Frisbee," Coadwell says. He and Heather came back to Brevard permanently the next year.

"Moving was an adventure. It didn't need a lot of planning. I come from a family of immigrants. My parents moved from Great Britain to New Zealand on their own, leaving their family in the 1950s," Coadwell

Kiwi Gelato serving gelato and sorbetto in Brevard. *Author's collection.*

says. "New Zealanders need to get out of their box. It's a small country. So traveling and moving are a rite of passage to get a better understanding of the planet."

"While I was waiting for a work visa, I used the time to dream. What could I add to the area?" Coadwell thought. He felt that Americans did not know how to drink coffee properly, but maybe another coffee shop in Brevard might not work. He got the idea of gelato after a lot of driving around Western North Carolina.

When Coadwell came to Brevard, no one was offering gelato. He felt it was different enough from ice cream. "You need to be mindful of how you impact other businesses," Coadwell says. "I was not going to place myself next door to an ice cream parlor."

Gelato in Italian means frozen. The frozen dessert actually goes back to Louis XIV, who gave an Italian chef the exclusive right to sell gelato in France. Gelato has less butterfat than ice cream, making the flavor more intense. There's also less air in gelato so you get more per cup.

Coadwell found PreGel, an Italian company in Charlotte that teaches entrepreneurs to make gelato and sells gelato-making equipment. The two-day course was free at the time. "So Heather and I took it. Heather was teaching in the local schools at the time," Coadwell says.

George Williams of Downtown Chocolates in Times Arcade Alley had some free space that became Kiwi Gelato's first home. "I really didn't really know what I was doing. Heather and I tried to run the business in 110 square feet. It was not a great location because visitors didn't wander down the alley," Coadwell remembers. "I could see them look down the alley and trying to decide if it was worth walking the extra steps for a couple of shops. They'd turn around and continue on Main Street." Locals might frequent his business, but visitors wouldn't venture there.

"In 2010, this spot on East Main Street became available. I didn't want to be too close to other shops making ice cream," Coadwell says. Kiwi Gelato is decorated in all things New Zealand. Kiwi birds in wood or stuffed cuddly toys are on his shelves along with books and maps. Photos of the South Island adorn his walls. The Kiddie Corner offers puzzles and games.

"This is the best gelato in Brevard made by a New Zealander," Coadwell says. "I make it the way I want to make it." Coadwell uses Italian machines with Italian ingredients. He was trained by an Italian company and takes periodic refresher courses. Since 2008, Coadwell also sells gelato at the Brevard Music Center in the summer, where he brings two roll carts.

There have been constant changes to Brevard. He and his family, now with an eleven-year-old son, live less than two miles from downtown. "Businesses come and go. People retire or are no longer enthusiastic. In 2010, most of this block was empty."

He's also seen changes at DuPont Forest. "We used to go to Fawn Lake and were the only people there. It was like our private lake. Now the parking and the lake are packed," Coadwell says. But the growth of DuPont Forest and Pisgah National Forest are good for business because visitors spend money in the county.

Now, most of his business is impulse purchases from visitors. "Lots of people here still dream of quieter days, but we need nonresidents. Even Ingles Supermarket does."

"Do you go back to New Zealand?" I ask Coadwell. "I go back as often as I can, but not as much as I like. I miss the food—green lip mussels and Bluff oysters."

Coadwell spends time with another full-blooded New Zealander in the area who also has a son. The four of them watch rugby, a big sport in their home country. "I miss my family," Coadwell says. "I left my sister to deal with our aging parents."

"Brevard is pretty good," Coadwell says. "You get stuck into the area. We're not surrounded by busy roads. Our basic needs are met. I coached soccer at my son's school." Coadwell was president of Heart of Brevard, part of a national association that supports and revitalizes downtown. It puts on many festivals. "As a small town, we need to work together."

And what is a tip jar doing on his counter? New Zealanders are known for not tipping for any service. Their employees get paid a good wage without tips. "I didn't have a tip jar," Coadwell says. "But people kept leaving money on the counter. So I put in a tip jar. It reminds me that I'm working in the United States."

MARIELLE DEJONG COMES HOME

Marielle DeJong came of age in the new Brevard. She moved to the area from Atlanta when she was in the third grade in 2000. Her parents did not want to raise her and her older sister in a city environment. The family chose Brevard because it was about an hour away from each set of grandparents.

The Future of DuPont Forest

"My dad is self-employed, and my mom became a fifth-grade teacher in the Brevard school system. She still teaches the same grade," DeJong says. When she mentally scrolls down her group of high school friends, she remembers that most of their parents worked in local government, construction industry or the allied health field.

When she was growing up, she recalls, "No one talked about the DuPont Corporation closing. Everyone talked about Ecusta." Dr. Adrian Miller, her eighth-grade math teacher, had worked in a lab at Ecusta. He now teaches at Blue Ridge Community College, the area's community college, at the same institution as Marielle's sister, Annalise. "The Ecusta plant, located just off the main highway into Brevard, seemed right there in the periphery, when you went to BI-LO Supermarket or to Asheville. I even learned to drive in the Ecusta parking lot, long after it was shuttered."

"I learned nothing about local history in school," DeJong recalls. "I learned about DuPont and Pisgah National Forests from friends who were introduced to the outdoors by their parents."

DeJong knew that she was always headed for college. Because she was a good student at Brevard High School, she went to UNC–Chapel Hill on a prestigious scholarship. By her own admission, she was not quite ready for Chapel Hill, either academically or socially. "There were about eight hundred students in Brevard High School when I graduated. High school teachers probably knew who you were before the first day of class. There were no college counselors tailored to me," she explains. Starting in the sixth grade, she was with the same twenty students until graduation. She was blown away by academics in college. "Tourism may have blossomed in Brevard by the time I went to high school, but not the education system. The high school didn't have the same sophistication as the restaurants and art gallery."

This phenomenon, that small-town students have a harder time in large universities, has been acknowledged by educators, even as they encourage college attendance and completion. Parents are also concerned that their children will not come back to the area if they go away to college. When Jeff McDaris went to high school in Brevard, high school graduates could walk right into a job at either DuPont Corporation or Ecusta. McDaris, now superintendent of Transylvania County schools, says many of his classmates went to college in Research Triangle, Charlotte or Atlanta and never returned to Transylvania. "That's true; there's a brain drain," he noted in a recent *Asheville Citizen-Times* article.

"Most of my friends went to state colleges, some to community colleges, some to work in the construction or service industry," DeJong says. Marielle DeJong graduated with honors from UNC–Chapel Hill, but she did return home. After a prestigious internship, she is now the event manager at Friends of Great Smoky Mountains National Park in Asheville.

Today, Brevard and Transylvania County are without major industry. But the outdoors, summer camps, new restaurants and gathering places bring in visitors, second homeowners and new residents. That's where the bulk of the jobs will be.

CONTEMPLATIONS AND SPECULATIONS

What would have happened to the land if DuPont Corporation had not bought it in 1956? DuPont Corporation purchased more than ten thousand acres from two main landowners, Frank Coxe and Alex Guion. At the time, there is no evidence that either landowners was actively looking for buyers. We can assume that they took the opportunity when it came along. But what if DuPont Corporation had not come along? Several former employees speculate:

> JEFF JENNINGS: "I imagine that the land would look a lot like much of the other mountainous land in Transylvania County. Look at the aerial photos of the land of waterfalls, lots of private homes and developments and occasional farm near waterfalls—say look specifically at the area between DuPont Forest, Jocassee and Brevard/Rosman…this land is not dissimilar in many regards, but it is chewed up into hundreds of small parcels, which lowers that land's potential in terms of conservation and public use."
>
> CHUCK RAMSEY: "There would be a small series of housing developments in the 1970s. By then, developers would have seen how successful Connestee Falls was."
>
> BILL THOMAS: "That's an interesting question. I don't think it would have become a state forest without DuPont Corporation. What could the DuPont land have become if the company hadn't bought it? Summer camps, trailer park, development, housing…"

The Future of DuPont Forest

>   SKIP (ARNOLD) SHELTON: "In 1956, it wasn't that easy to sell this quantity of land. There were no roads or infrastructure. Sure, by the 1970s, developers would have come in to build on the site."

In 1956, 10,000 acres was a large amount of land; it still is. Summer camps and church retreats were popular in Western North Carolina at the time but would not have used that much land. Sherwood Forest, a 1,000-acre housing estate on US 276 in Cedar Mountain, was created in 1957 by a couple from Columbia, South Carolina. Connestee Falls, another large development on the same road, dates from the early 1970s. A survey taken of fifty summer camps in the area in 2014 reported that the average camp size is only 399 acres. The segregated South of the 1950s was not the attractive area it is now. The Coxe and Guion land would have sat untouched for a long while before it was all absorbed into various uses.

Fast-forward to the twenty-first century. By the end of 2000, DuPont Forest was intact. DuPont Forest is not the latest piece of private land that became public in North Carolina. Chimney Rock State Park in Rutherford County has been a private tourist attraction since the 1880s. Jerome Freeman bought land from the Speculation Company, owned by the Coxes, the same family that eventually sold Buck Forest land to DuPont Corporation. The two parcels of land included the rock and a waterfall, both very desirable attractions. Freeman conceived of a tourist attraction when he built a trail to the base of the chimney and a stairway to the top.

The next owner, Dr. Lucius Morse, bought Chimney Rock in 1902. He built the bridges, roads and trails that are mostly used today. An elevator was added in 1949 to get visitors to the top of the rock. When Chimney Rock was put up for sale in 2006 by the Morse family, the public did not waste any time asking Governor Mike Easley to save the rock. It became a state park the next year. The park still charges an admission because of its high maintenance features.

Grandfather Mountain State Park also has roots in private family ownership. In 1888, Hugh MacRae bought a tract of land that included Grandfather Mountain from W.W. Lenoir, son of the Revolutionary War soldier and politician. Hugh Morton, grandson of the original owner, developed the land into a commercial success, building the Swinging Bridge and Nature Museum. Morton also put in place a series of conservation easements that forever protects the Grandfather Mountain backcountry from development.

When Hugh Morton died in 2006, his heirs promised to keep Grandfather Mountain in its natural state. The North Carolina State Park system bought more than 2,400 acres, which it designated the backcountry and turned into Grandfather Mountain State Park. The land with the attractions is managed by the Grandfather Mountain Stewardship Foundation, a nonprofit organization that charges an admission fee. Did the history of DuPont Forest spur the creation of these new parks?

DUPONT FOREST CONTINUES TO GROW

In the eastern United States, public land has always come from private sources, whether donated, sold or abandoned. Private veteran groups have protected battlefield sites since the American Revolution. When people started visiting these places in large numbers, the groups realized that they could not adequately oversee the public and safeguard the resources. They turned the land over to the federal or state government.

DuPont Forest is no different; in this case, the land was sold to the North Carolina Forest Service. Recently, the forest grew by another 402 acres with the donation from the Picklesimer estate. And more land may be coming from the Continental Divide tract. The Eastern Continental Divide separates the waters flowing east toward the Atlantic from those flowing into the Gulf of Mexico. This land, located south of DuPont Forest, links the forest to more than 100,000 acres of public land along the North Carolina–South Carolina state line, including Jones Gap State Park, Caesar's Head State Park and several other wilderness areas.

The link to other conserved land is as important as the actual acreage. It will be a while until people can explore this new land because it needs to be surveyed and studied for endangered and protected species. How will this land be used? For more trails? Will there be parking for visitors? Or will it be left alone as just protected land? A plan needs to be put in place.

But plants and animals have no such restrictions; they are not waiting for a written management plan to be approved by the state. They can move about between seasons and increase their range as the climate changes. Wildlife corridors increase the population and diversity of animals, which cuts down on inbreeding.

Visitors are coming from all over the country and even the world. Whether you accept the prediction of a million visitors in 2020 or the 862,000 visitors

The Future of DuPont Forest

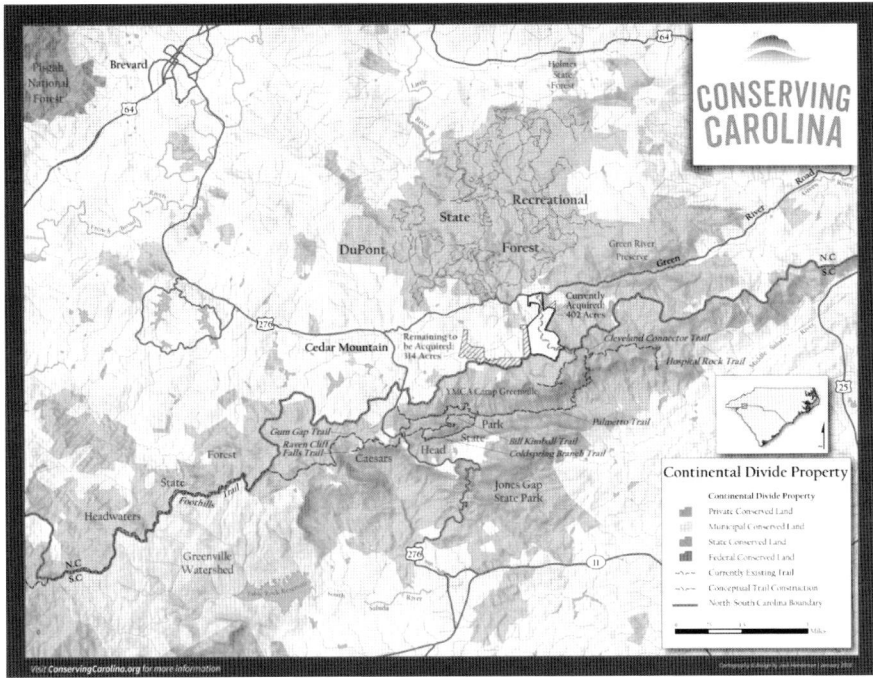

Continental Divide tract is located south of the forest in Transylvania County and extends across the Eastern Continental Divide. *Courtesy of Conserving Carolina.*

cited in annual legislative report for fiscal year 2019, it's a lot of people for a small state forest. At the beginning, everyone wanted more visitors to enjoy the forest. That goal has been accomplished.

In the year 2000, when the public got an intact forest, Friends of DuPont Forest became the nonprofit organization that supports DuPont Forest. It offers volunteer crews to repair trails and funds specific projects in the forest.

Trails are affected by all the love and attention they're getting. DuPont Forest officially closes single-track trails when the conditions are too wet and muddy for feet, hooves and wheels. Visitors can use gravel roads when single-track trails are closed. The forest gets the word out with press releases and social media. Although there's no enforcement, outdoor clubs make it a point of pride to follow the edict.

With five access areas, users can spread out. Hooker and High Falls Access Areas are always the most popular because the waterfalls are so close and so are the bathrooms, another major draw. Maybe a differential entrance fee can encourage visitors to discover other parts of the forest.

Eventually, the donut hole, where DuPont Corporation is still cleaning up, will be open to the public, adding more acreage to the useable part of the forest. Lake DERA, now behind the fence in the donut hole, might become available to the public as a real swimming lake. That will attract a new group of visitors.

The DuPont Corporation and its successors have long left their manufacturing roots in Brevard. The forest belongs to everyone: newcomers, longtime locals and visitors from across the state or the world. Although the forest has existed for more than two decades, it's still a teenager—growing, spreading out, sometimes loud and crowded and sometimes quiet, solitary and thoughtful.

Today, as I climb Stone Mountain from Guion Farm, I see no one—nobody on the trail, nobody on top. Maybe it's because the trail descriptions say that it's a strenuous hike; bikers will have to push their bikes or leave them at the bottom. Stone Mountain is at the extreme northeast corner of the forest. I'm on an exposed granite slab enjoying the southern views as I explore the top while eating a few cookies. Vegetation is pushing up in the cracks in the stone. A short trail to the left offers an even better panorama. This is my forest and yours as well.

Bibliography

Adams, Kevin. *North Carolina Waterfalls*. Winston-Salem, NC: John F. Blair, 2016.
Agreement to Join Buck Forest Club. Lease between Frank Coxe and Buck Forest Club. March 24, 1947. Transylvania County Library, Rowell Bosse North Carolina Archives.
Arthur, John Preston. *Western North Carolina: A History, 1730–1913*. Spartanburg, SC: Reprint Company, 1973.
Asheville Area Chamber of Commerce and Asheville Real Estate Board. *Live and Invest in the Land of the Sky*. Frank Coxe Collection, D.H. Ramsey Library, Special Collections, University of North Carolina–Asheville.
Axell, Nathaniel H. "State to Improve Safety at DuPont Forest." Blue Ridge Now, May 16, 2020. blueridgenow.com.
Bayne, Bruce, and Christian Hauser. *DuPont Brevard Ecological Inventory Summary Report*. Pioneer Technologies, October 20, 2011, revised January 27, 2016. uspioneer.com.
Better Living Magazine. "Any Day of the Week" (May/June 1967).
———. "New Faces in Town" (May/June 1958).
Boggs, W.G. "Silicon and Its Uses." Unpublished memo, October 24, 1957. Transylvania County Library, Rowell Bosse North Carolina Archives.
Bond, Amelia Yancey. Personal interview by telephone, October 2018.
Brown, Dave. Personal interview by telephone, January 2020.
Brown, Jerry. "Cemeteries Provide Clues to Forest's Past." *The Little River Watermark*, Friends of DuPont Newsletter, January 2015.

Bibliography

Burgess, Joel. "DuPont Deal Still Up in the Air." Blue Ridge Now, April 1, 2005. blueridgenow.com.

———. "Plant Won't Reopen." *Times News*, July 29, 2005.

Byrd, Caitlin. "Downtown Brevard 'in the Midst of a Rebirth.'" *Asheville Citizen-Times*, December 5, 2014. citizen-times.com.

Capital at Play. "Summer Camps in Western North Carolina." May 2014. capitalatplay.com.

Carden, Gary. "The Kingdom of the Happy Land." *Smoky Mountain Living*, September 1, 2009.

Carney, John. *History of the Property Acquisition*, n.d. Transylvania County Library, Rowell Bosse North Carolina Archives.

———. "Hooker-Moore Cemetery History." Friends of DuPont Newsletter, December 2011.

———. *Notes of Triple Falls Murder*, n.d. Transylvania County Library, Rowell Bosse North Carolina Archives.

Cart, Ben. *The Best of All Worlds*. Brochure for Buck Forest Residential Property, n.d. Transylvania County Library, Rowell Bosse North Carolina Archives.

Chavez, Karen. "Doughnut Hole Closes for DuPont State Recreational Forest." *Asheville Citizen-Times*, January 22, 2017. citizen-times.com.

———. "DuPont State Forest Starts New Year with More Conservation Land." *Asheville Citizen-Times*, January 5, 2018. citizen-times.com.

———. "DuPont State Recreational Forest Might See Entry Fees under New Bill." *Asheville Citizen-Times*, April 10, 2019. citizen-times.com.

———. "Timber Harvest Planned at DuPont State Recreational Forest." *Asheville Citizen-Times*, August 3, 2018.

———. "Where Are All the People at Holmes State Educational Forest?" *Asheville Citizen-Times*, April 5, 2017. citizen-times.com.

Clawson, Lucas C. "The British Are Coming! (Aren't They?): Defending Wilmington in the War of 1812." Hagley Museum & Library Research and Collection News, February 7, 2013. hagley.org.

Coadwell, Richard. Personal interview, Brevard, North Carolina, December 2019.

Corn, Connie Hubbard. Personal interview, Brevard, North Carolina, June 2018.

Coyle, John H., III, Corporate Valuation Associates. "Five Tracts of Potential Excess Land Adjoining the Brevard Plant of E.I. du Pont de Nemours and Company Transylvania and Henderson Counties, Brevard, North Carolina." November 12, 1986. Transylvania County Library, Rowell Bosse North Carolina Room Archives.

Bibliography

Daddio, Jess. "The Summer Camp Effect." Blue Ridge Outdoors, May 12, 2018. blueridgeoutdoors.com.

———. "Wheels and Waterfalls: Mountain Biking DuPont State Forest." Blue Ridge Outdoors, March 15, 2004. blueridgeoutdoors.com.

De Bona, Beth. "What Is that? Historic Cemetery in DuPont." Blue Ridge Now, January 20, 2016. blueridgenow.com.

DeJong, Marielle. Personal interview, Bryson City, North Carolina, December 2019.

Delwiche, Bob. "Hyper Pure Silicon." Unpublished memo, August 13, 1997. Transylvania County Library, Rowell Bosse North Carolina Archives.

———. Personal interview, Hendersonville, North Carolina, December 2018, January 2019.

DeWitt, Dan. "Endangered or Not? An Elusive Salamander Makes a Controversial Comeback." Blue Ridge Outdoors, May 18, 2009. blueridgeoutdoors.com.

Diagnostic Imaging. "Agfa Completes Sterling Purchase." June 1, 1999. diagnosticimaging.com.

———. "Du Pont Medical Imaging Unit Evolves into Sterling Diagnostic Imaging." April 10, 1996. diagnosticimaging.com.

Dickson, Joan. Personal interview, Asheville, North Carolina, December 2018.

Dickson, John. Personal interview, Brevard, North Carolina, October 2018.

Dinkins, Geraldine. "Aleen Steinberg: Lover of Nature, Preserver of Lands." Go Upstate, June 30, 2014. goupstate.com.

Du Mont, Brian M. *Ecusta and the Legacy of Harry Straus*. Baltimore, MD: Publish America, 2007.

DuPont Photo Products Department. "Brevard Plant." Unpublished booklet written for the tenth anniversary of the film plant, 1972. Transylvania County Library, Rowell Bosse North Carolina Archives.

DuPont Pigments Department. "DuPont Hyperpure Silicon for Semiconductor Devices." Unpublished booklet, n.d. Transylvania County Library, Rowell Bosse North Carolina Archives.

Durden, Robert, F. *Electrifying the Piedmont Carolinas: The Duke Power Company, 1904–1997*. Durham, NC: Carolina Academic Press, 2008.

Dykeman, Wilma. *The French Broad*. New York: Henry Holt and Company, 1955.

Easley, Michael. Letter to everyone who wrote to him about saving the DuPont waterfalls, November 1, 2000. Private correspondence.

Ellison, George. "Admiration, Maybe, but No Love for the Boar." *Smoky Mountain News*, April 28, 2010. smokymountainnews.com.

Bibliography

Elliston, Jon, and Kent Priestley. "The Kingdom of the Happy Land." *Mountain Xpress*, February 7, 2007.

English, Stuart. Personal interview, Brevard, North Carolina, January 2020.

Fay, Susan. Personal interview, Hendersonville, North Carolina, February 2020.

Fotofax. "Charlie Paxton Recounts History of Plant Property." October 1977.

———. "Don Blankenship, 'Mr. First,' Remembers." October 1977.

———. "Lewis Says…We Need a Better Road to Du Pont." March 1970.

Garren, Kit, and Marilyn Garren. Personal interview, Cedar Mountain, North Carolina, January 2020.

Gastonia Gazette. A.H. Guion & Company General Contractor advertisement. April 24, 1914.

Gordon, Brian. "Fewer NC Rural Students Go to College. Educators Are Working to Close the Gap." *Asheville Citizen-Times*, December 15, 2019.

Graham, William. Personal interview, Brevard, North Carolina, December 2019.

Greenawalt, Bruce. Interview with Frank Coxe, June 6, 1979. D.H. Ramsey Library Special Collections. toto.lib.unca.edu/findingaids/oralhistory/SHRC/coxe_frank.pdf.

Griffin, Marty. Personal interview, Brevard, North Carolina, December 2019.

Guidry, Jason. Personal interview, Brevard North Carolina, January 2020.

Haines, Brian R. "Frequently Asked Questions About the Donation of the 476-Acre Property to DuPont State Recreational Forest." North Carolina Forest Service, n.d. ncforestservice.gov.

Hale, Meg. "DuPont State Forest offers Certification for Pack Llamas." Blue Ridge Now, April 6, 2007. blueridgenow.com.

Henderson Times-News. "Friends of the Falls. World Class." Advertisement, March 2000.

Hirsch, Alan. Personal interview on the telephone. February 2020.

Hubbard, Channing. Personal interview, Hendersonville, North Carolina, April 2018.

Jacober, Diane. Personal interview, Arden, North Carolina, May 2018.

Jennings, Elizabeth. "New Supervisor Begins Job at DuPont." Blue Ridge Now, October 6, 2013. blueridgenow.com.

Jennings, Jeff. "Buck Forest Hunt Club History: Interview with Bill Duckworth." September 1, 2001. Transylvania County Library, Rowell Bosse North Carolina Room Archives.

———. "Buck Forest Hunt Club History: Interview with Joshua Camblos." September 25, 2005. Transylvania County Library, Rowell Bosse North Carolina Room Archives.

Bibliography

———. Personal interview, Arden, North Carolina, April 2018.

Johnson, Earle. Personal interview, Brevard, North Carolina, November 2018.

Kays, Holly. "Here to Stay: Coyotes Make Themselves at Home in WNC." *Smoky Mountain News*, February 17, 2016. smokymountainnews.com.

Keen, Woody. "Don't Compromise the DuPont State Forest." *Mountain Xpress*, September 6, 2000.

Kelly, Susan Stafford. "Tiny but Mighty." *Our State Magazine* (December 2019).

Kerns, Charlie. "NC Waterfalls Make Movie Appearance in 'Max.'" Go Upstate, July 5, 2015. goupstate.com.

Knoll, Rosemarie Shannon. *Wildflowers and Waterfalls of DuPont State Forest*. North Carolina: High Falls Publishing, 2016.

Kudva, Ashok. Personal interview, Hendersonville, North Carolina, April 2018.

LaBar, Ryan "Squirrel." "Bike Magazine Hits DuPont State Forest." *Bike Magazine* (October 6, 2011). bikemag.com.

Lacey, Derek. "Fees Proposed for DuPont Forest to Help Manage Growth." Blue Ridge Now, April 20, 2016. blueridgenow.com.

———. "Sen. Chuck Edwards Introduces Bill for DuPont Forest Fee Study." Blue Ridge Now, April 7, 2019. blueridgenow.com.

Lancaster, Lindsay. "Unearthing History." Blue Ridge Now, April 8, 2007. blueridgenow.com.

Lane, Rose Jenkins. "The Kingdom of the Happy Land." Conserving Carolina. conservingcarolina.org.

Lemon, Cindy. *Hiking DuPont State Recreational Forest*. N.p.: self-published, 2016.

Lutz, Sara Lela. "Growing Hope: Perspectives on Development in a Southern Appalachian County." Master's thesis, School of International Service of American University, April 23, 2007.

Markets Insider. "DowDuPont™ Merger Successfully Completed." Press release, September 1, 2017. markets.businessinsider.com/news/stocks/dowdupont-merger-successfully-completed-1002301589.

McCotter, Ellen. Personal interview, Asheville, North Carolina, October 2018.

McGrady, Chuck. Personal interview, Hendersonville, North Carolina, January 2020.

McGraw, Amy, B. "Forest Access through Agfa Property Cut Off." Blue Ridge Now, January 19, 2002. blueridgenow.com.

Bibliography

Meanix, Nancy. "The Story behind School Integration." Blue Ridge Now, February 20, 2005. blueridgenow.com.

Meinzer, Chet. Personal interview, Cedar Mountain. December 2019.

Metzger, Harrison. "Agfa Plant to Close." Blue Ridge Now, February 27, 2002. blueridgenow.com.

———. "DuPont Waterfalls a Site for All." Blue Ridge Now, December 12, 2010. blueridgenow.com.

———. "Explore the Beauty Next Door." Blue Ridge Now, May 28, 2004. blueridgenow.com.

———. "Octogenarian Ranger Retires." Blue Ridge Now, May 22, 2004. blueridgenow.com.

———. "Public to Own Waterfalls." *Times-News*, October 24, 2000.

———. "State Deposits Money for Falls." *Times-News*, October 25, 2000.

———. "State Officials Vow to Take Waterfall Land." *Times-News*, October 19, 2000.

———. "Upstate Developer Proceeding as State Eyes Land Acquisition." *Times-News*, October 20, 2000.

———. "Wildlife Federation Honors Friends of Falls." Blue Ridge Now, February 10, 2001. blueridgenow.com.

———. "Workers Dismantle Plant to Clear Land for Park's Use." Blue Ridge Now, March 9, 2006. blueridgenow.com.

Morrison, AB. "Brevard Plant Tract Cedar Mountain Transylvania County North Carolina." DuPont Corporation memo, October 25, 1962. Transylvania County Library, Rowell Bosse North Carolina Archives.

———. "DuPont Corporation Memo to All Employees Regarding the First Satisfactory Roll of Film." October 21, 1963. Transylvania County Library, Rowell Bosse North Carolina Archives.

Morrow, Mac. Personal interview, Brevard, North Carolina, November 2018.

Muller, John D. "Letter from Caesar's Head, South Carolina." July 15, 1894. Transylvania County Library, Rowell Bosse North Carolina Archives.

Mundhenk, Andrew. "DuPont Forest to Grow by 753 Acres After Picklesimer Donation." Blue Ridge Now, January 12, 2018. blueridgenow.com.

———. "DuPont Visitation Stabilizes, but Trash, Vandalism Increases." Blue Ridge Now, April 16, 2019. blueridgenow.com.

North Carolina General Assembly. *Article 74. Acquisition and Control of State Forests and State Recreational Forests*. ncleg.gov.

———. *Senate Bill S390—North Carolina*. ncleg.gov.

Orr, Barbara Johnson. Personal interview, Henderson County, North Carolina, September 2019.

Bibliography

Parker, Keith. *Seven Cherokee Myths: Creation, Fire, the Primordial Parents, the Nature of Evil, the Family, Universal Suffering and Communal Obligation*. Jefferson, NC: McFarland & Company, 2005.

Patton, Sadie Smathers. *The Kingdom of the Happy Land*. Asheville, NC: Stevens Press, 1957.

Pioneer Technologies Corporation. "Conceptual Remedial Action Plan. DuPont Brevard Site." February 6, 2016. files.nc.gov/ncdeq/Waste%20Management/DWM/HW/Dupont/Draft%20Brevard%20Conceptual%20RAP_02_05_16.pdf.

Ramsey, Chuck. Personal interview, Brevard, North Carolina, May 2018.

Reed, Betty J. *The Brevard Rosenwald School: Black Education and Community Building in a Southern Appalachian Town, 1920 to 1966*. Jefferson, NC: McFarland, 2015.

Reed, Christian. *The Land of the Sky: Adventures in Mountain By-Ways*. Alexander, NC: Land of the Sky Books, 2001.

Richardson, Kathy Brittain, and Marcie Hinton. *Applied Public Relations: Cases in Stakeholder Management*. New York: Routledge Communication Series, 2015.

Richie, Al. Personal interview, Asheville, North Carolina, November 2018.

Riddle, Lyn. "Battle Over Developing a Scenic Mountain Tract." *New York Times*, January 14, 2001.

———. "North Carolina Mountain Tract Fuels Controversy." *Baltimore Sun*, January 26, 2001.

Roe, Kieran. Personal interview, Asheville, North Carolina, January 2020.

Rowell Bosse North Carolina Room. "A to Z Tour of Transylvania County." July 25, 2016. nchistoryroom.blogspot.com/2016/07/summit-camps-airstrip.html.

———. "Bridal Veil Falls a Destination for Travelers." October 10, 2019. transylvaniatimes.com.

———. "Buck Forest Hotel Preceded DuPont in Cedar Mountain." March 31, 2014. nchistoryroom.blogspot.com.

———. "Cedar Mountain: A True Summer Community—Cedar Mountain NC." April 7, 2014. nchistoryroom.blogspot.com.

———. "Cedar Mountain Has Been Home to Several Camps." July 6, 2015. nchistoryroom.blogspot.com.

Ruscin, Terry. "Beyond the Banks: The History of DuPont State Forest." Blue Ridge Now, April 9, 2018. blueridgenow.com.

———. *Hidden Secrets of Henderson County North Carolina*. Charleston, SC: The History Press, 2013.

Bibliography

Schmid, J.R. "Natural Heritage Program." Memo to J.H. Golden, plant manager, August 9, 1984. Transylvania County Library, Rowell Bosse North Carolina Archives.

Schneider, Brian J. *DuPont State Forest Land and Resource Management Plan*. DuPont State Recreational Forest, June 2011. dupontstaterecreationalforest.com.

Shelton, Ken. "Preserve Access to Waterfalls." *Henderson Times-News*, March 25, 2000.

Shelton, Skip (Arnold). Personal interview, Hendersonville, North Carolina, April 2019.

Snyder, John. *Hill of Beans: Coming of Age in the Last Days of the Old South*. Kittery Point, ME: Smith/Kerr Associates, 2011.

Sprouse, Vicki. "Savoring Summer." *The Scribe's Pen* (blog), July 18, 2009. thescribespen.wordpress.com/tag/lake-dera.

Steinberg, Aleen. Personal interview, Cedar Mountain. June 2018.

Stewart, Kevin G., and Mary-Russell Roberson. *Exploring the Geology of the Carolinas: A Field Guide to Favorite Places from Chimney Rock to Charleston*. Chapel Hill: University of North Carolina Press, 2007.

Summerville, Diane. "Searching for the Elusive Flicker of Blue Ghost Fireflies." *Our State Magazine* (August 2011).

Summit Camps. Brochure, n.d. Transylvania County Library, Rowell Bosse North Carolina Archives.

Summit Camps Application, 1977. Transylvania County Library, Rowell Bosse North Carolina Archives.

Taylor, Marcia. "40 Years: A Scrapbook of Holmes Educational State Forest." Blue Ridge Now, May 24, 2017. blueridgenow.com.

Thomas, Bill. Personal interview, Cedar Mountain, North Carolina, May 2018.

Thompson, Marcy. "Cascade Power Began Operation in 1909." Blue Ridge Now, March 3, 2014. blueridgenow.com.

———. "DuPont Started as Silicon Plant." *Transylvania Times*, April 14, 2014.

———. "Ecusta Christmas." Rowell Bosse North Carolina Room, December 9, 2019. nchistoryroom.blogspot.com/2019/12/ecusta-christmas.html.

Todd, Mark. "Agfa to Close Doors." Blue Ridge Now, September 13, 2002. blueridgenow.com.

———. "Agfa Workers Leave for the Last Time." Blue Ridge Now, November 28, 2002. blueridgenow.com.

Transylvania Heritage Museum. "Solomon Jones, the Road Builder." Poster on wall.

Bibliography

Troxler, Steve. *Annual Legislative Report on DuPont State Recreational Forest.* October 1, 2019. Transylvania County Library, Rowell Bosse North Carolina Archives.

Van Buskirk, Jamie. Personal interview by telephone, December 2019.

Van Noppen, Ina W., and John J. Van Noppen. *Western North Carolina Since the Civil War.* Boone, NC: Appalachian Consortium Press, 1973.

Walter, Rebecca. "Local Company Equilibar's Products Part of NASA's Artemis Program." Blue Ridge Now, September 29, 2019. blueridgenow.com.

Wilcox, Kent. "DuPont Proposes Remediation of the Donut Hole." *The Little River Watermark*, Friends of DuPont Newsletter, July 2016. dupontforest.com.

———. "Summit Airstrip Was Built for Business and Pleasure." *The Little River Watermark*, Friends of DuPont Newsletter, April 2015, July 2015.

———. "Where Does the Water Come From?" *The Little River Watermark*, Friends of DuPont Newsletter, October 2015, January 2016.

Woolard, Edgar. *Dear Caroline, Dear Will: Letters to My Grandchildren.* Wilmington, DE: Woolard Associates, 2005.

Zilg, Gerard Colby. *DuPont: Behind the Nylon Curtain.* New York: Prentice Hall, 1974.

Index

A

Agfa 74, 116, 119, 123, 127, 129, 130, 131, 136, 156, 157
Anthony, Jim 116, 117, 119, 120, 121, 122

B

bikers 15, 42, 113, 114, 117, 118, 123, 131, 137, 138, 142, 143, 144, 146, 148, 153, 166, 176
Brown, David 86, 133, 134, 135, 146, 148
Buck Forest Hotel 27, 28, 30, 31, 37
Buck Forest Lodge 18, 21, 22, 37, 40, 41, 42, 14, 58, 99

C

Cart, Ben 18, 93, 94, 95, 96, 97, 98, 100, 102, 103, 116, 146
Corn, Connie Hubbard 63, 105
Coxe, Frank 18, 22, 28, 37, 38, 39, 41, 46, 47, 51, 56, 67, 69, 71, 172, 173

D

donut hole 119, 133, 155, 156, 160, 176
du Pont, E.I. 53, 54

E

Easley, Mike 118, 119, 120, 121, 173

INDEX

Ecusta 50, 51, 60, 61, 63, 78, 88, 90, 106, 107, 108, 109, 131, 171
equestrians 15, 84, 117, 118, 134, 138, 142, 143, 145, 146, 148

F

Fay, Susan 160, 161, 163
Fotofax 60, 71

G

Guidry, Jason 135, 148, 149, 150, 160
Guion, Alex 18, 47, 48, 49, 51, 56, 67, 172, 173
Guion Farm 28, 46, 47, 48, 49, 65, 67, 68, 70, 71, 84, 112, 114, 128, 148, 176

H

Hirsch, Alan 117, 119, 120, 121
Holmes Educational State Forest 48, 106, 160, 161, 163
Holmes, John Simcox 48, 161
Hubbard, Channing 61, 62, 63, 105, 136
Hunger Games, The 135, 149, 155, 159

J

Jennings, Jeff 110, 118, 120, 121, 123, 127, 128, 129, 172
Johnson, Earle 50, 67, 68, 75, 76, 77, 78, 89, 106

L

Last of the Mohicans, The 117, 153, 154

M

McGrady, Chuck 110, 111, 112, 117, 128, 142
Meinzer, Chet 117, 154, 155, 156, 157, 159
Morrison, AB 66, 67, 68, 69, 70, 73

P

Paxton, Charlie 70, 71, 109, 114

S

segregation 50, 51, 61, 77, 78
silicon 56, 64, 66, 69, 77, 88
Staton, Lewis 82, 83
Staton Road 27, 44, 63, 73, 79, 81, 83, 88, 112, 130, 135, 137, 154

Steinberg, Aleen 96, 118, 121, 122, 123, 124
Sterling Diagnostic 109, 110, 112, 116, 122, 128, 129, 131, 133

T

Thomas, Micajah 27, 28, 29, 146

X

X-ray 59, 66, 71, 72, 73, 74, 78, 103, 127, 128, 129

About the Author

Danny Bernstein is a hiker, hike leader and outdoor writer. She's been a committed hiker since her early twenties, having completed the Appalachian Trail, all the trails in Great Smoky Mountains National Park, the South beyond 6000 peaks, the Mountains-to-Sea Trail across North Carolina and three Caminos de Santiago. She currently leads hikes for Carolina Mountain Club, Friends of the Smokies and the Asheville Camino group.

She's written two Southern Appalachian hiking guides, *The Mountains-to-Sea Trail Across North Carolina*, published by The History Press, and *Forests, Alligators, Battlefields: My Journey through the National Parks of the South* to celebrate the 100th anniversary of the National Park Service.

In her previous life, she worked in computer science, way before computers were cool, first as a software developer and then as a professor of computer science. Her motto is "No place is too far to walk if you have the time."

Visit us at
www.historypress.com